THANK YOU !

LAURENCE KING, JO LIGHTFOOT, ANGUS HYLAND,
IDA RIVEROS, SARAH BATTEN, FELICITY AWDRY
GIOVANNA CELLINI, CLARE PRICE, LAURA CARLIN,
LIZZIE FINN, SARAH HOLLYWOOD, IZZIE KLINGELS,
ABIGAIL SMILEY-SMITH, FERGUS PURCELL,
SARAJANE CROSSLEY,
GEMMA RYAN, CHRISTIAN PETERSEN,
ALLY WHALLER, CLARE SHILLAND,
and
BEN BRANAGAN

CREDITS

(IN ORDER OF APPEARANCE)

ANDRÉ PERUGIA

LEA STEIN

JUDITH LEIBER – www.judithleiber.com

HERMÈS – www.hermes.com

JEAN DESSÈS

THEA CADABRA – www.theacadabra.com

JUDY BLAME

MARIANO FORTUNY – www.fortuny.com

COMME DES GARÇONS.
SHOES FROM THE 2009-10 A/W COLLECTION –
www.comme-des-garcons.com

COUSIN ITT © CHARLES ADDAMS.

WITH PERMISSION TEE and CHARLES
ADDAMS FOUNDATION –
www.charlesaddams.com

OH, JUST ONE LAST THING ...

DESIGN the INVITE FOR YOUR FASHION SHOW

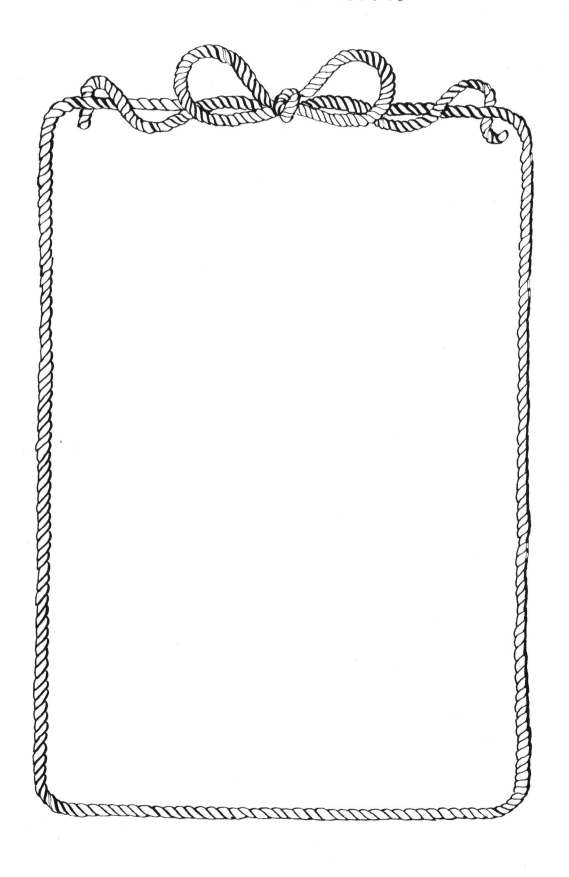

WHO WOULD YOU INVITE TO YOUR FASHION SHOW?

GUEST LIST

1. -----------------------

2. -----------------------

3. -----------------------

4. -----------------------

5. -----------------------

6. -----------------------

7. -----------------------

8. -----------------------

9. -----------------------

10. -----------------------

EXTRA SPECIAL V.I.P. GUEST

... OR PIN ONE TO A HAT

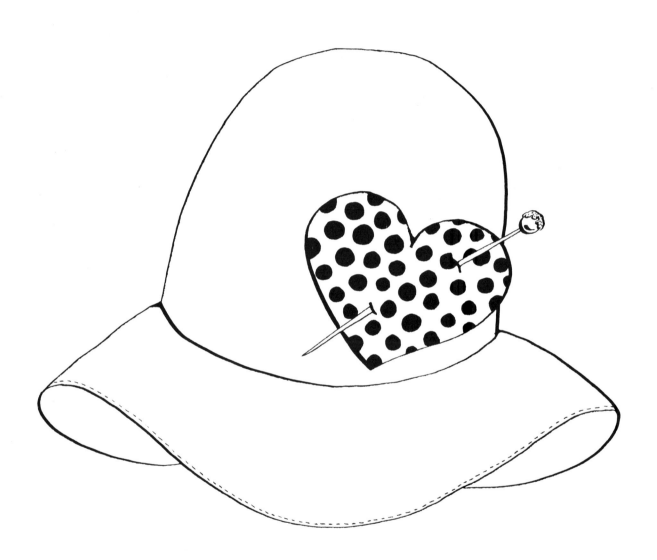

HOW ABOUT SEWING ONE OF THE HEARTS ONTO A JEAN POCKET?

...VOILÀ, A NEW BAG IS BORN !

CUT OUT HEARTS FROM SCRAPS OF FABRIC

SNIP SNIP SNIP

and SEW OR GLUE THEM TO AN OLD CANVAS SHOPPER . . .

PAINT each HEART ♡ a DIFFERENT COLOUR AND CREATE A UNIQUE TEXTILE PATTERN

FILL THESE TOTE BAGS
WITH YOUR WONDERFUL DESIGNS

OLD SOUL, NEW SHOES
DRAW YOUR LATEST PAIR

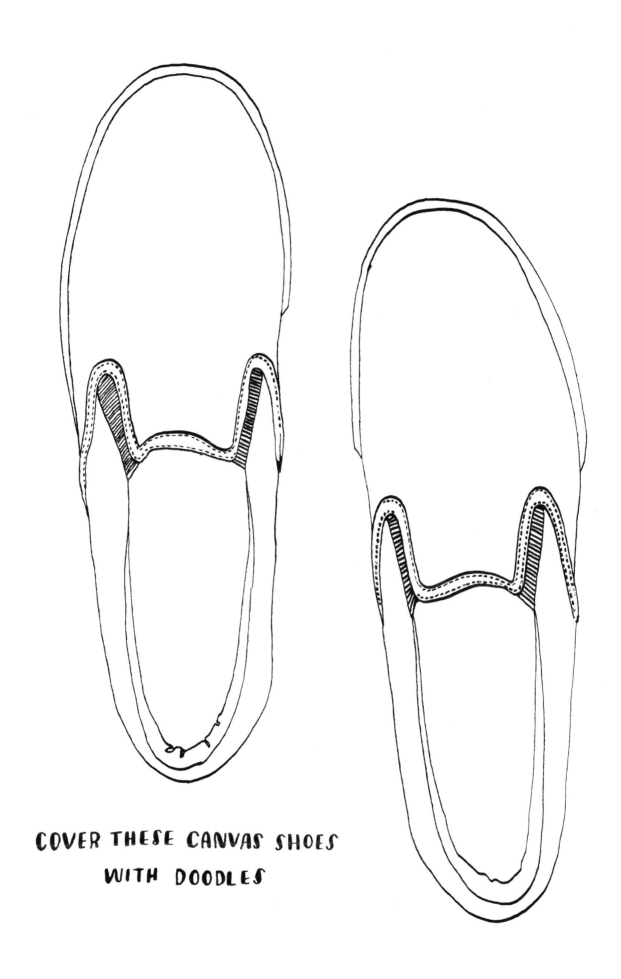

COVER THESE CANVAS SHOES
WITH DOODLES

DRAW A FACE TO GO WITH THESE LIPS

WHO IS WEARING THESE PRETTY SUNGLASSES ?

COVER THIS MASK WITH
SEQUINS, BEADS and
LOTS and LOTS
OF JEWELS

HAIR HERO

LOUISE 'LULU' BROOKS
WAS A SILENT MOVIE ACTRESS
WHO CREATED A STORM
WITH
THE BOB

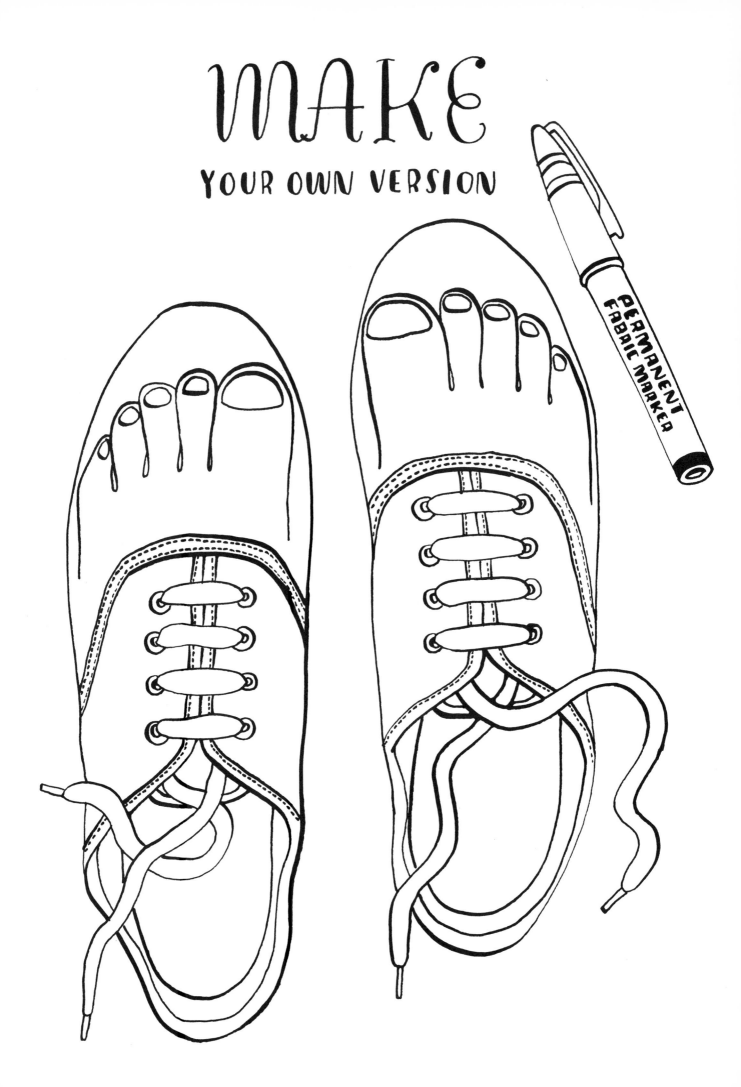

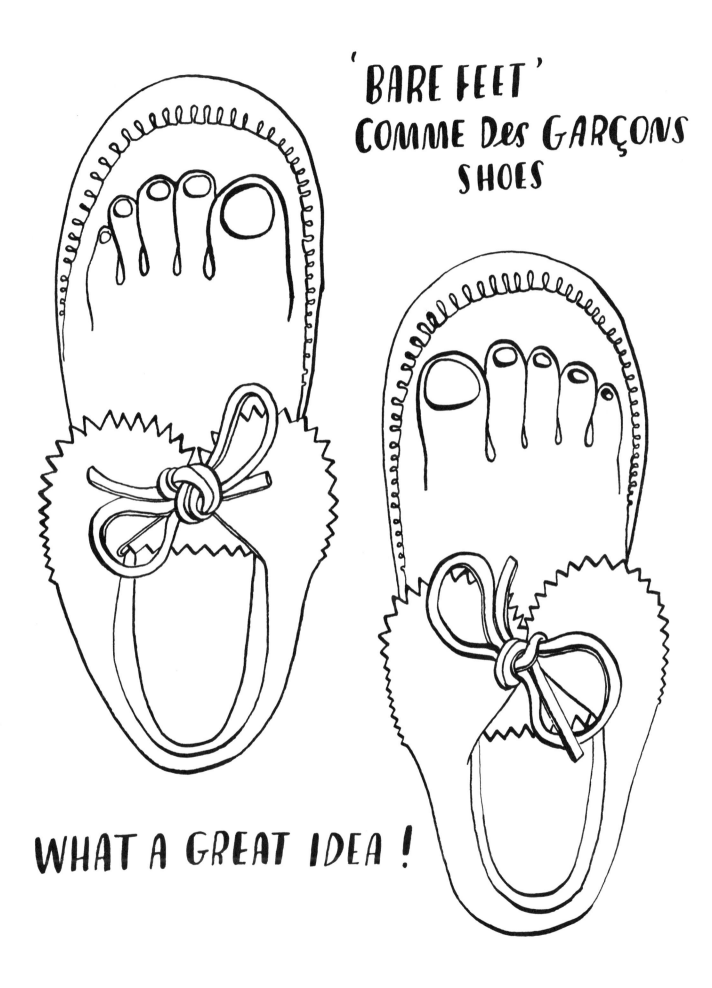

'BARE FEET'
COMME Des GARÇONS
SHOES

WHAT A GREAT IDEA !

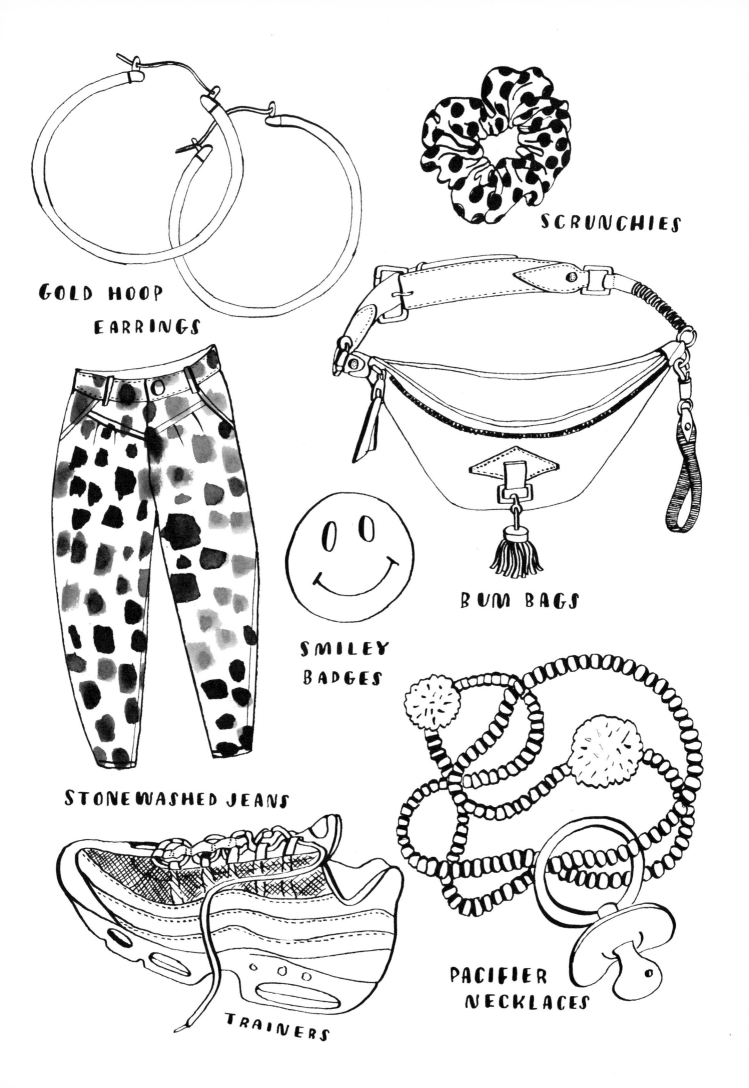

GOLD HOOP
EARRINGS

SCRUNCHIES

BUM BAGS

SMILEY
BADGES

STONEWASHED JEANS

PACIFIER
NECKLACES

TRAINERS

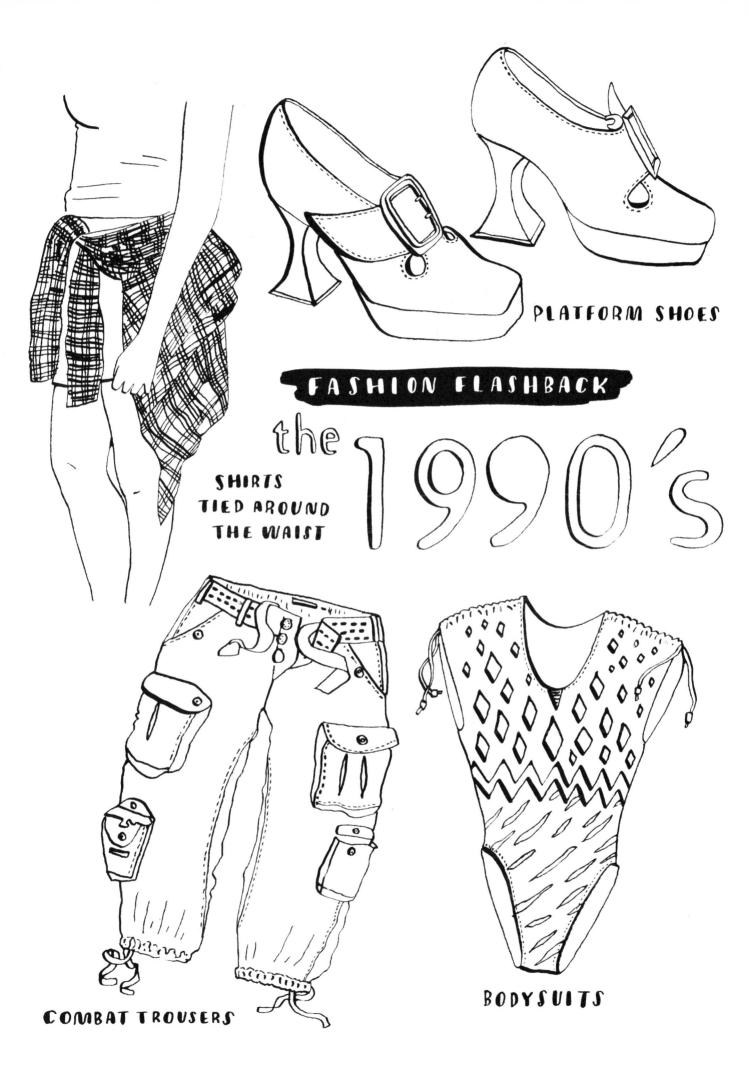

PLATFORM SHOES

FASHION FLASHBACK
the 1990's

SHIRTS TIED AROUND THE WAIST

COMBAT TROUSERS

BODYSUITS

DRAW the
MATCHING EARRING
        OR USE THE SPACE
                to CREATE YOUR
                        OWN DESIGN

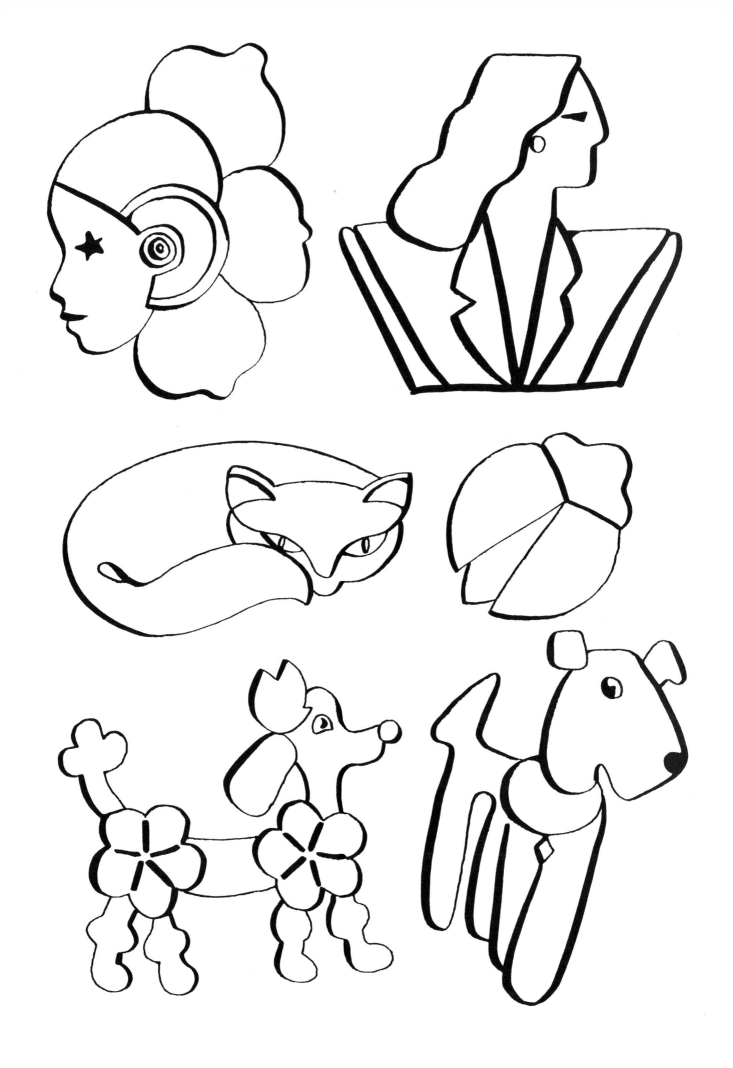

INVENT YOUR OWN
PATTERNS
FOR THESE
BEAUTIFUL LEA STEIN
BROOCHES

DRAW SOME CHARMING CHARMS
to COMPLETE THE BRACELET

CHARMED, I'M SURE

MAKE YOUR OWN UNIQUE NECKLACE BY THREADING TOGETHER CHAINS, CHARMS and TRINKETS

DRAW YOURSELF ON THIS PAGE
AND DRESS UP USING ANY OF THE
ITEMS ON THE PAGE OPPOSITE

BE an
OPULENT PEARLY QUEEN
AND DRAW MANY LAYERED STRANDS
OF PEARLS

DRAW THE BAG
ATTACHED TO THE HANDLE

HAVE FUN DRAWING HAIRSTYLES FOR THE LADIES

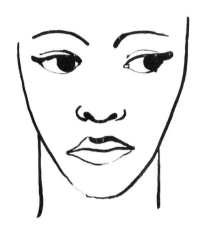

HAVE FUN DRAWING HAIRSTYLES FOR THE LADIES

DRAW WHAT COUSIN ITT LOOKS LIKE
UNDERNEATH ALL THAT HAIR

DRAW
SOME LONG,
DINGLY DANGLY TASSELS
HANGING DOWN FROM
THIS CAP

BE INVENTIVE

TURN
ORDINARY
CURTAIN TASSELS
INTO a SPLENDIFEROUS BELT

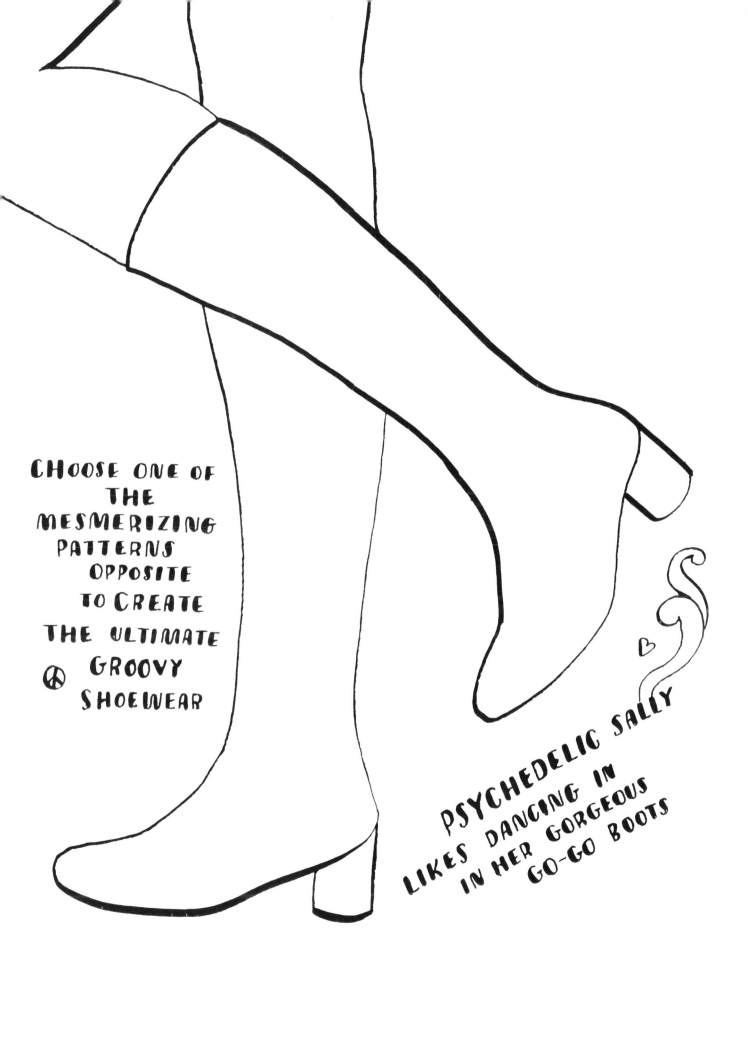

CHOOSE ONE OF THE MESMERIZING PATTERNS OPPOSITE TO CREATE THE ULTIMATE ☮ GROOVY SHOEWEAR

PSYCHEDELIC SALLY LIKES DANCING IN HER GORGEOUS IN HER GO-GO BOOTS

DRAW YOURSELF ON THIS PAGE
AND DRESS UP USING ANY OF THE
ITEMS ON THE PAGE OPPOSITE

WHAT WOULD YOU WEAR FOR A
FASHION HALLOWEEN ?

DRAW YOUR FANCY DRESS OF CHOICE HERE

FANGTASTIC NECKLACE !

...NOW IT'S YOUR TURN !

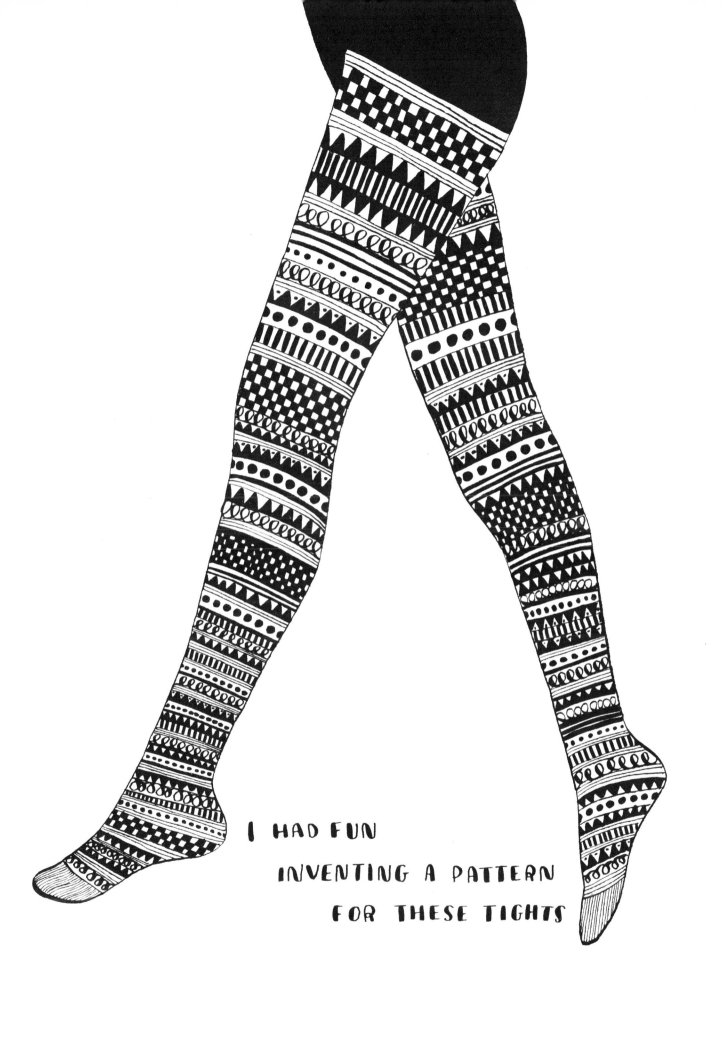

I HAD FUN
INVENTING A PATTERN
FOR THESE TIGHTS

EMBELLISH this BIB NECKLACE WITH
PRECIOUS GEMS, SEQUINS and BEADS

THE CHULLO HAT
COMES FROM
THE ANDEAN MOUNTAINS
AND DATES FROM PRE-HISPANIC TIMES

DRAW TALL FEATHERS
ONTO THIS MASK and
CREATE SOMETHING
ENCHANTING

BUCKSKIN, GLASS BEADS, THREADS, TALENT
and DILIGENCE ALL WENT INTO
MAKING THIS INCREDIBLE DRESS

1870

HAND CRAFTED BY THE LAKOTA TRIBE, NORTH AMERICA

DRAW YOURSELF ON THIS PAGE
AND DRESS UP USING ANY OF THE
ITEMS ON THE PAGE OPPOSITE

DRAW THE BAG
DANGLING AT THE
END OF THE CHAIN

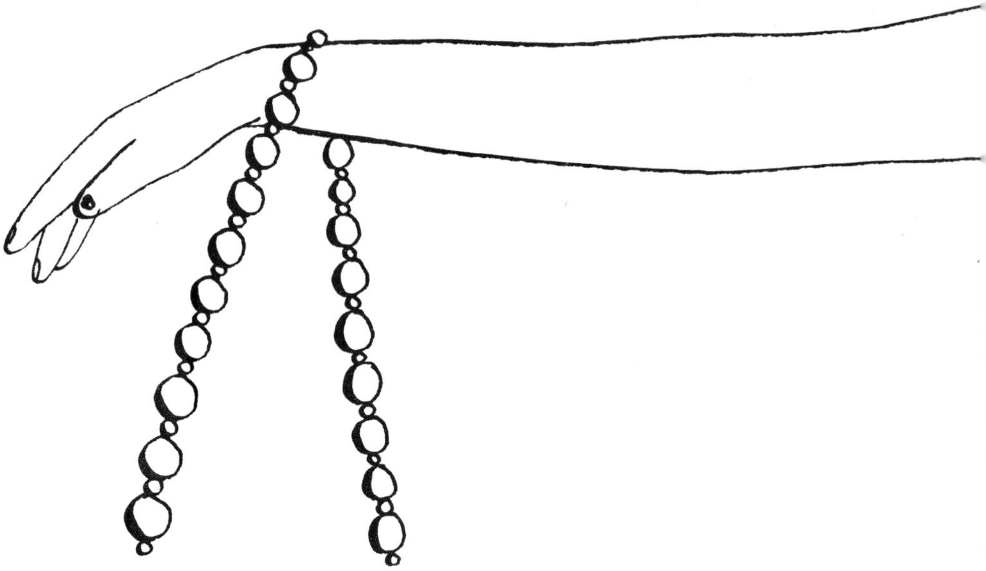

MAKE IT
BOLD,
MAKE IT
BEAUTIFUL

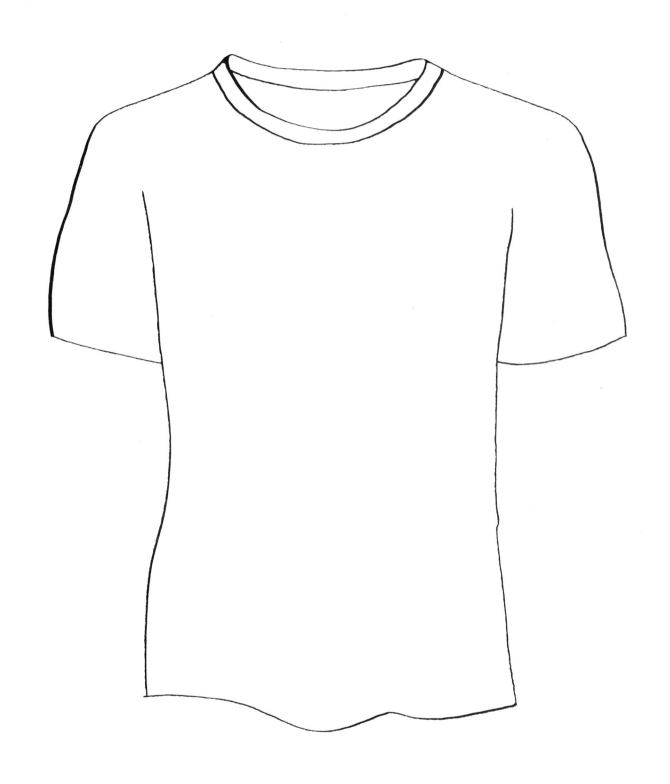

WRITE YOUR MOTTO

ON THIS T-SHIRT

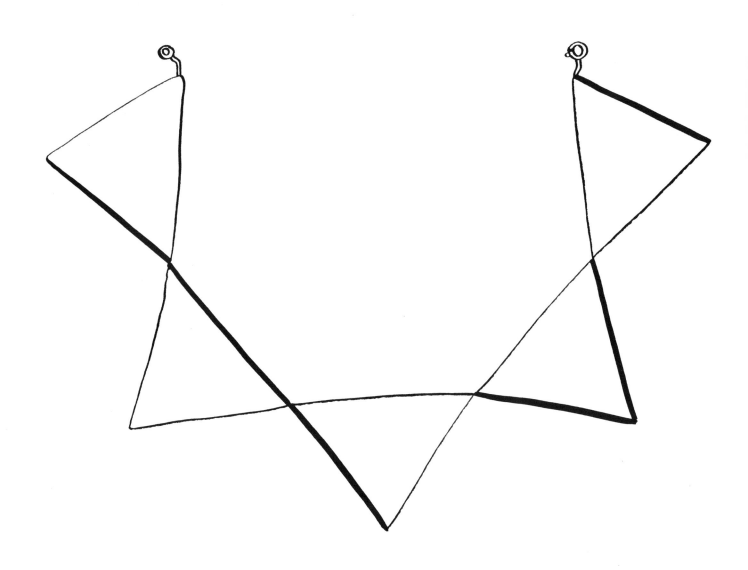

FILL THIS NECKLACE
WITH GEOMETRIC PATTERNS
and BEAUTIFUL COLOURS

DRAW SHOES THAT COULD FLY

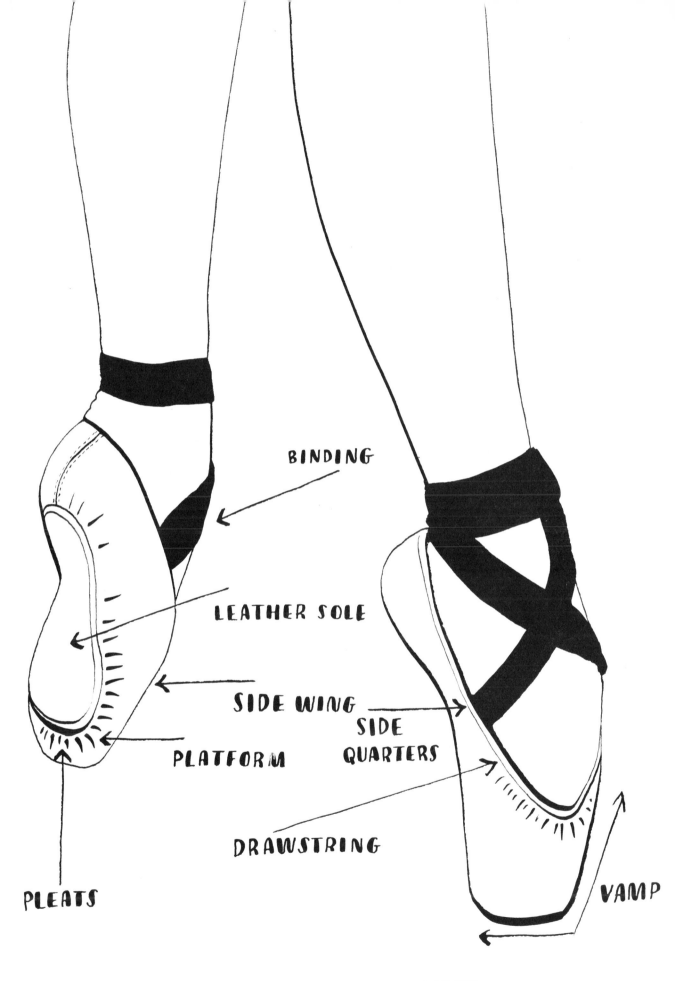

BINDING

LEATHER SOLE

SIDE WING

SIDE
QUARTERS

PLATFORM

DRAWSTRING

PLEATS

VAMP

ANATOMY OF A POINTE SHOE

DRAW THE BAG ATTACHED TO THIS WOODEN HANDLE

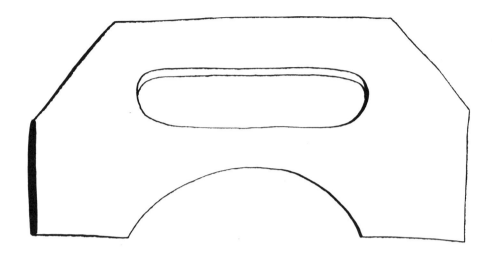

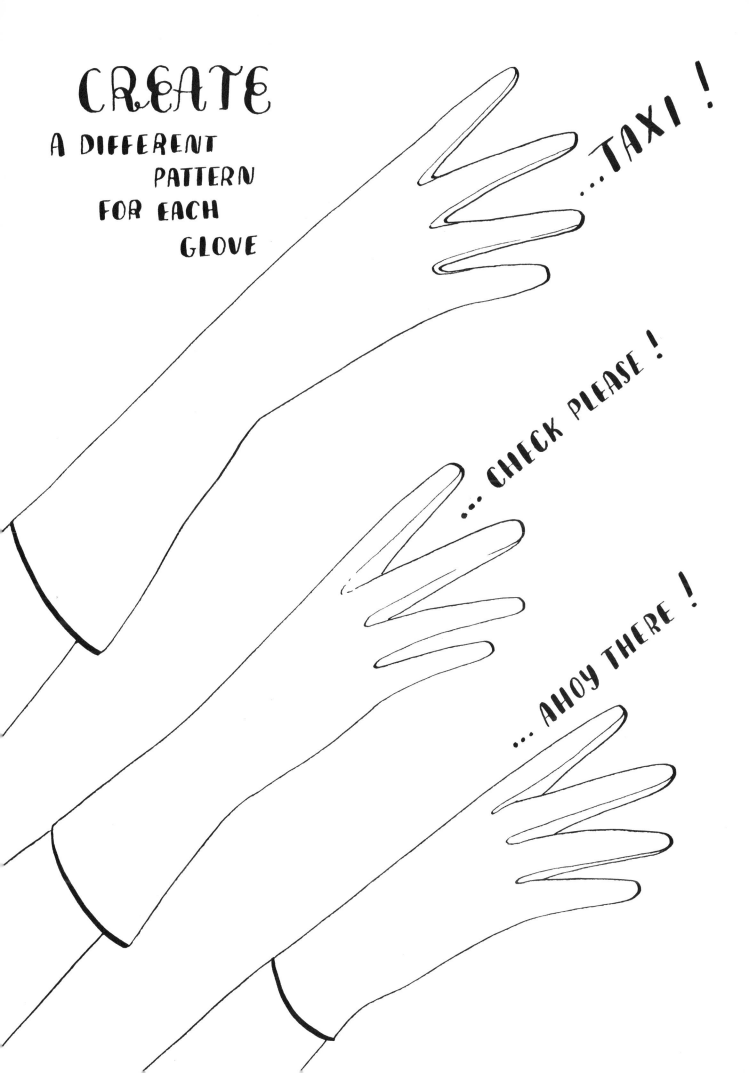

DRAW A FACE ON THIS PAGE
and ACCESSORIZE WITH
ANY OF THE ITEMS OPPOSITE

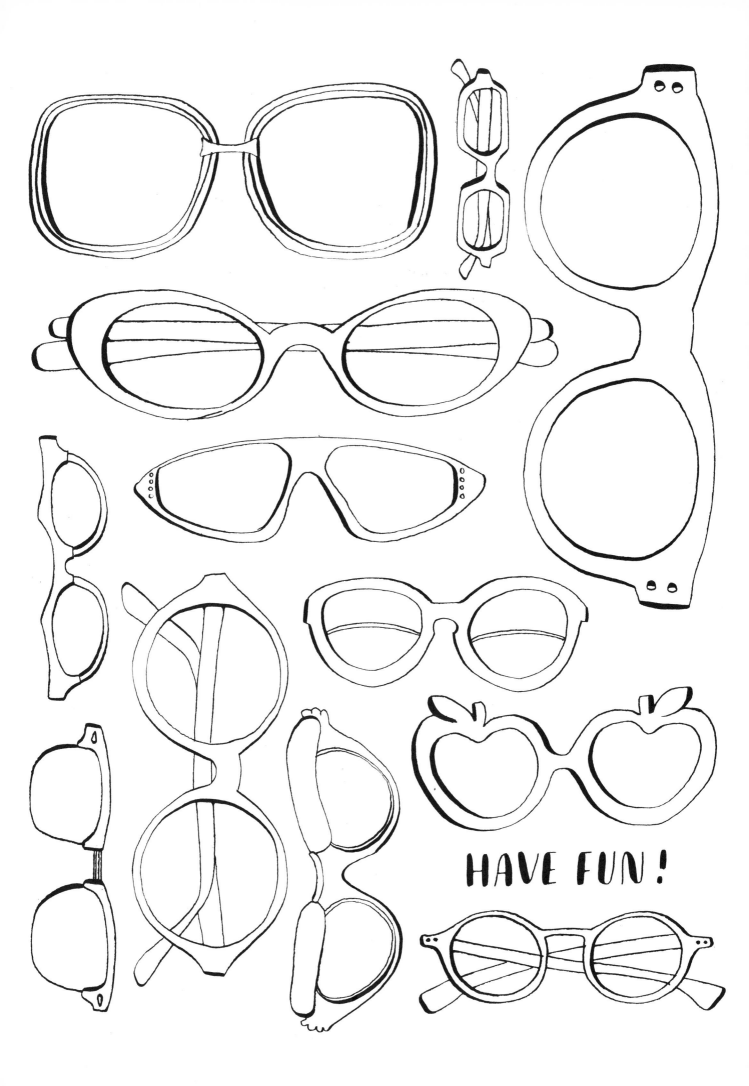

HAVE FUN!

EMBELLISH THESE FRAMES WITH SEQUINS, PRECIOUS GEMS and YOUR OWN PATTERNS

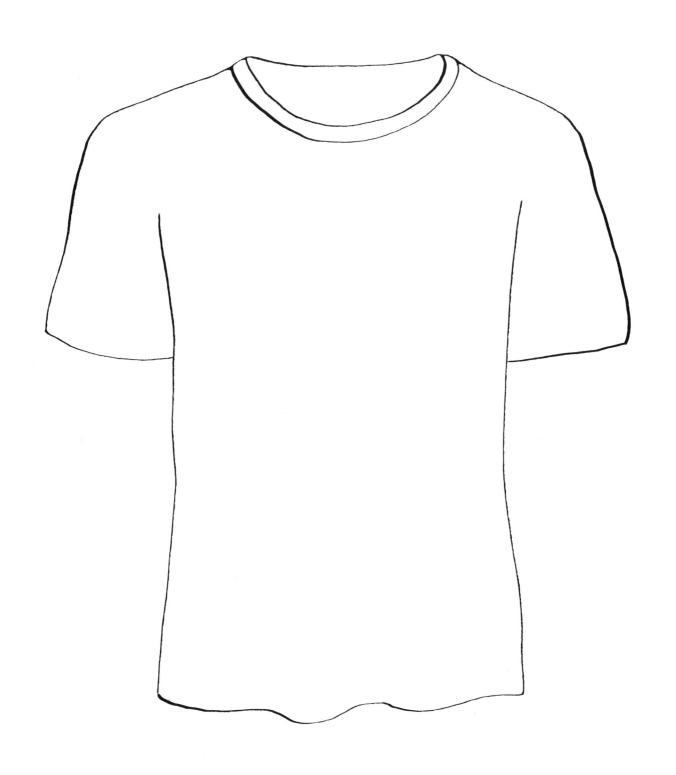

DRAW A BIG FLOWER
ON THIS T-SHIRT

HERE IS A T-SHIRT
FOR YOU TO DO WHAT
YOU LIKE WITH

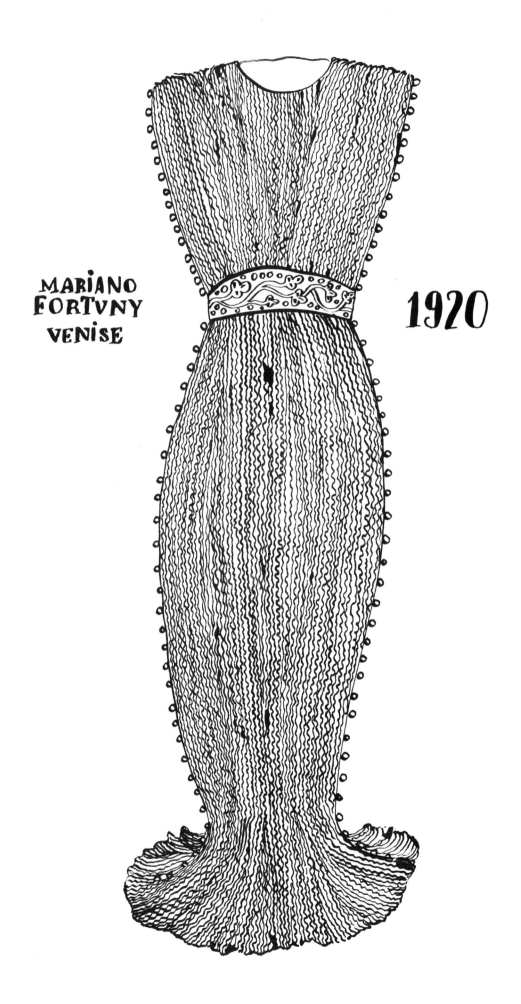

MARIANO
FORTVNY
VENISE

1920

the
GREEK
PEPLOS

420 B.C.

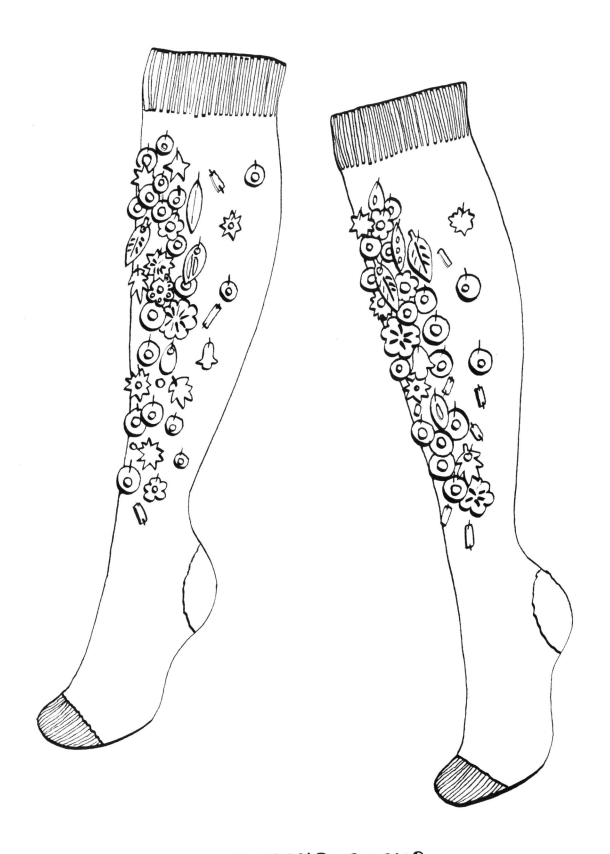

SPARKLE UP YOUR SOCKS
BY SEWING ON SEQUINS, BEADS
and BAUBLES

TRANSFORM THIS PLAIN SHIFT DRESS
BY DRAWING GEMS ONTO THE COLLAR

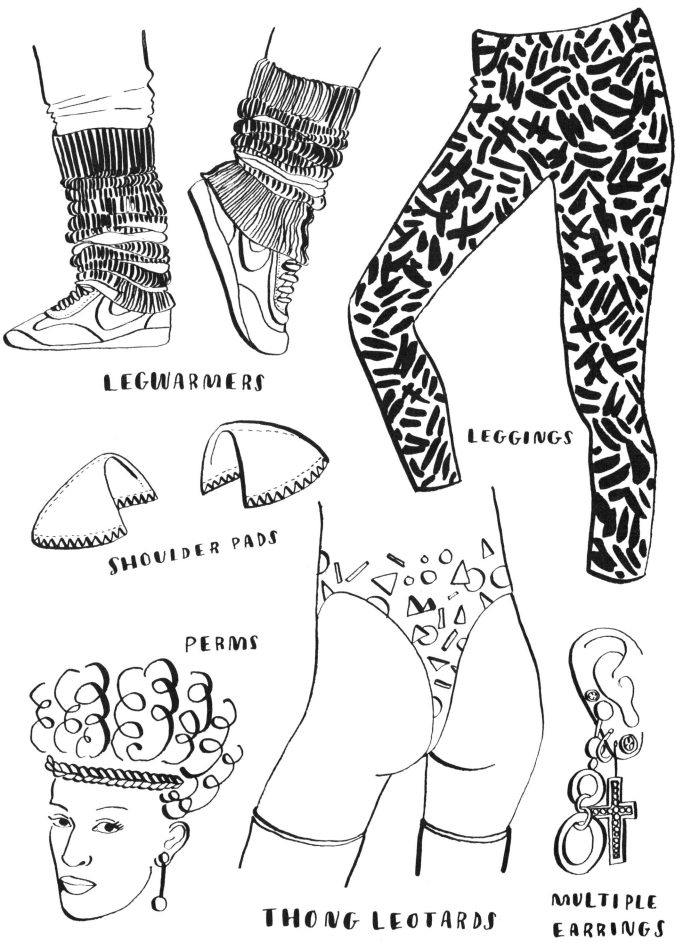

LEGWARMERS

LEGGINGS

SHOULDER PADS

PERMS

THONG LEOTARDS

MULTIPLE EARRINGS

HEADBANDS

SLOGAN T-SHIRTS

CHOOSE LIFE

CROP TOPS

PLASTIC JEWELLERY

FASHION FLASHBACK

the 1980's

GIANT BOWS

LACE GLOVES

COLOURS:
FLUORO PINK
FLUORO YELLOW
FLUORO GREEN
BLACK

COURT SHOES

GEOMETRIC SUNGLASSES

DESIGN A HAT INSPIRED BY PRINCESS LEIA'S HAIRSTYLE

MAY THE FORCE BE
WITH YOU

HAIR
HERO

PRINCESS LEIA AMIDALA SKYWALKER

DRAW THE COAT ATTACHED TO THIS COLLAR

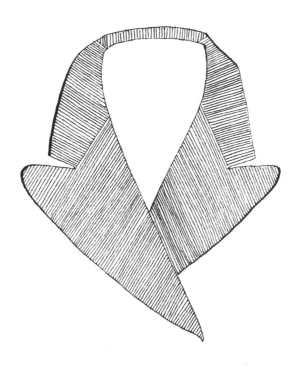

FASHION ARCHIVE

INSPIRED BY GONDOLIERS' HATS
THE 'BOATER' WAS CREATED in THE 1880's

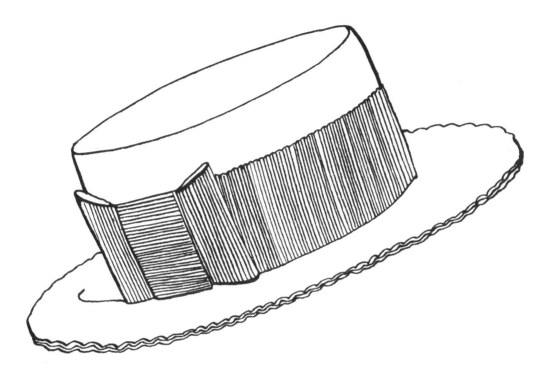

DRAW A JAUNTY GIRL
FOR THIS JAUNTY BOATER

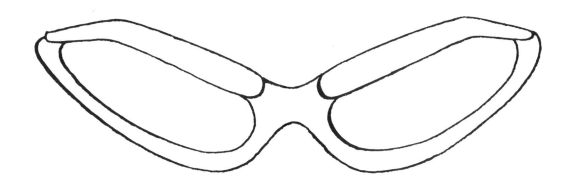

DRAW THE FACE BEHIND THESE SHADES

MAKE A NECKLACE FROM AN OLD LACE COLLAR

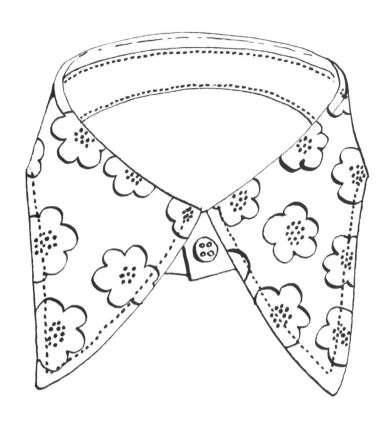

CUT COLLAR and CUFFS
FROM an OLD SHIRT
TO CREATE STYLISH
NEW ACCESSORIES

 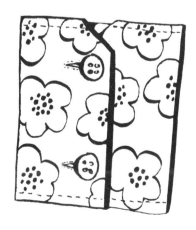

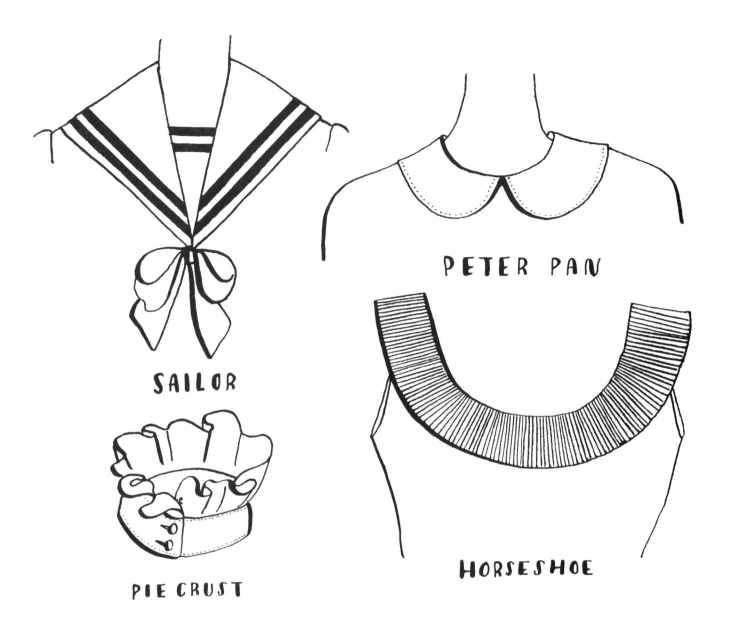

SAILOR

PETER PAN

PIE CRUST

HORSESHOE

... and EVEN MORE COLLARS !

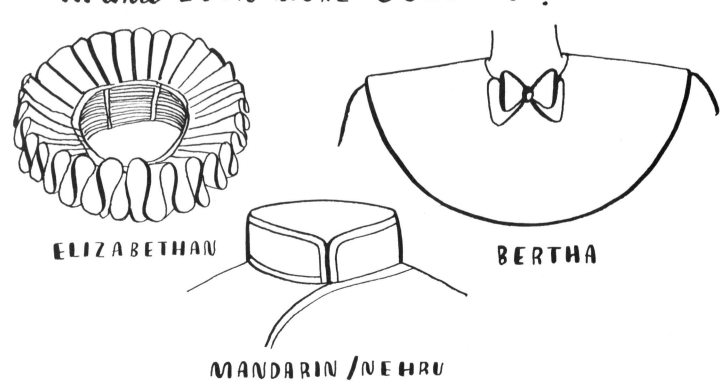

ELIZABETHAN

MANDARIN /NEHRU

BERTHA

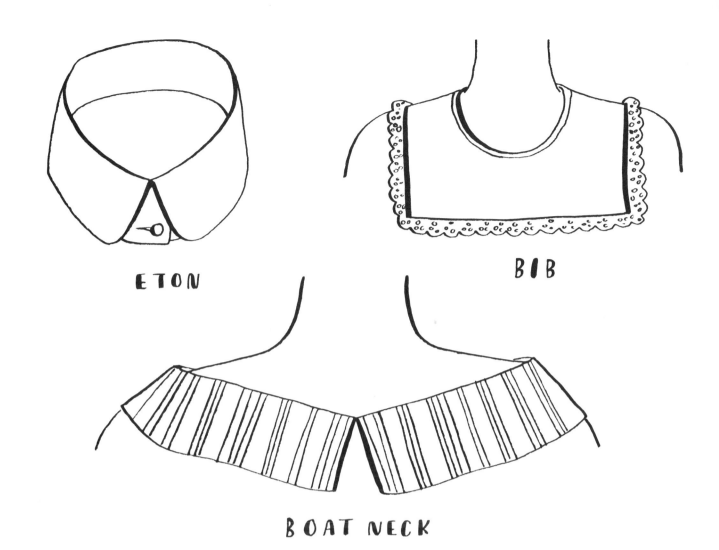

ETON

BIB

BOAT NECK

COLLARS ! COLLARS !

COLOUR IN AND ADD PATTERNS

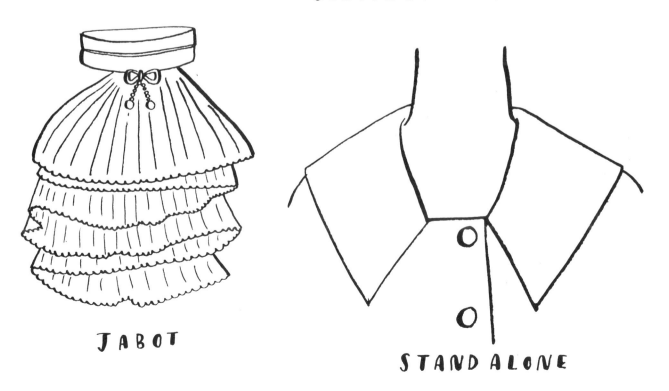

JABOT

STAND ALONE

DRAW...

A NECKLACE MADE OUT OF STARS

MAKE LIKE THE ANCIENT ROMANS and
FASHION YOURSELF A CROWN
OUT OF LEAVES

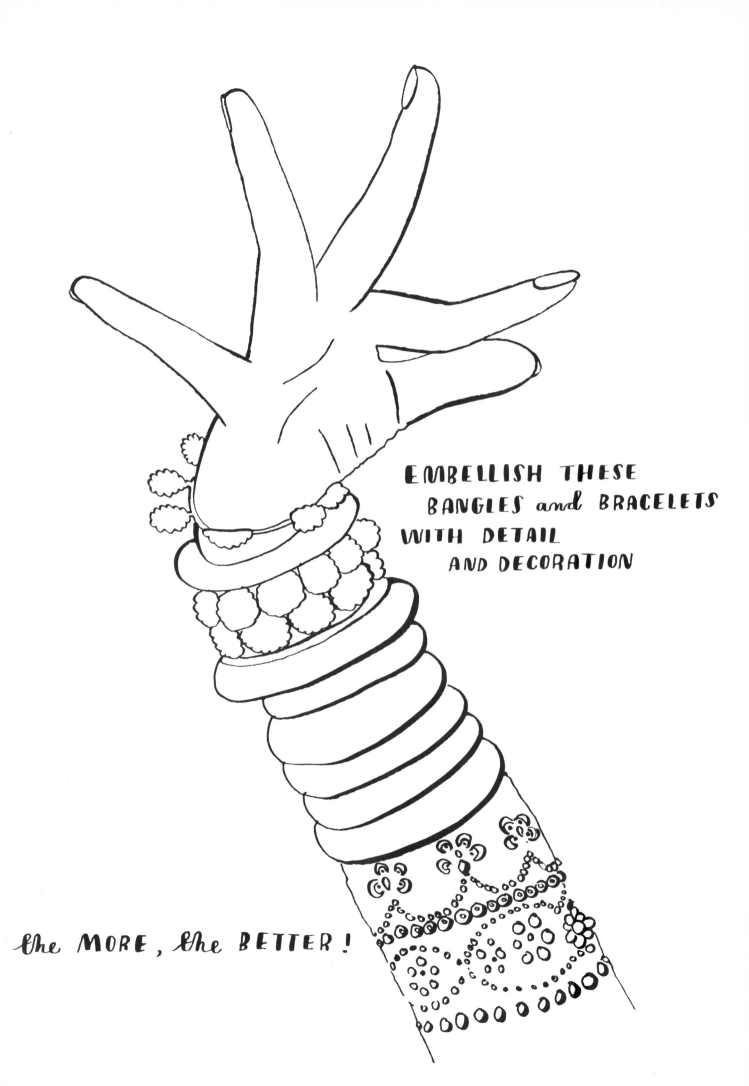

EMBELLISH THESE
BANGLES and BRACELETS
WITH DETAIL
AND DECORATION

the MORE, the BETTER!

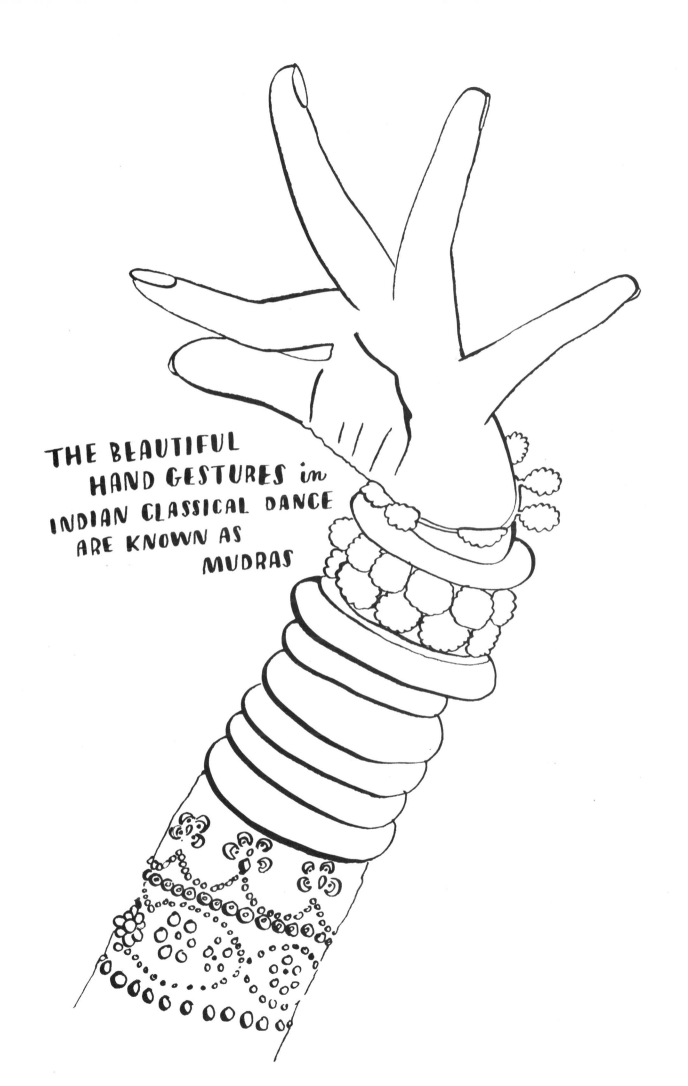

THE BEAUTIFUL
HAND GESTURES in
INDIAN CLASSICAL DANCE
ARE KNOWN AS
MUDRAS

DRAW EARRINGS THAT
MATCH BOTH
THE BANGLES and THE NECKLACE

GIVE THE NECKLACE
DIFFERENT PATTERNS
LIKE THE BANGLES

GLAM MAKE-UP

BIG SUNGLASSES

ROUNDED COLLARS

FLOPPY HATS

POLO NECKS

PLATFORM SHOES

HIGH WAISTED HOT PANTS

APPLIQUED BELT

FASHION FLASHBACK

the 1970's

COLOURS: ORANGE + BROWN

BELL BOTTOM JEANS

BOLD NATIVE AMERICAN JEWELLERY

CROCHET

FABRIC SWATCH

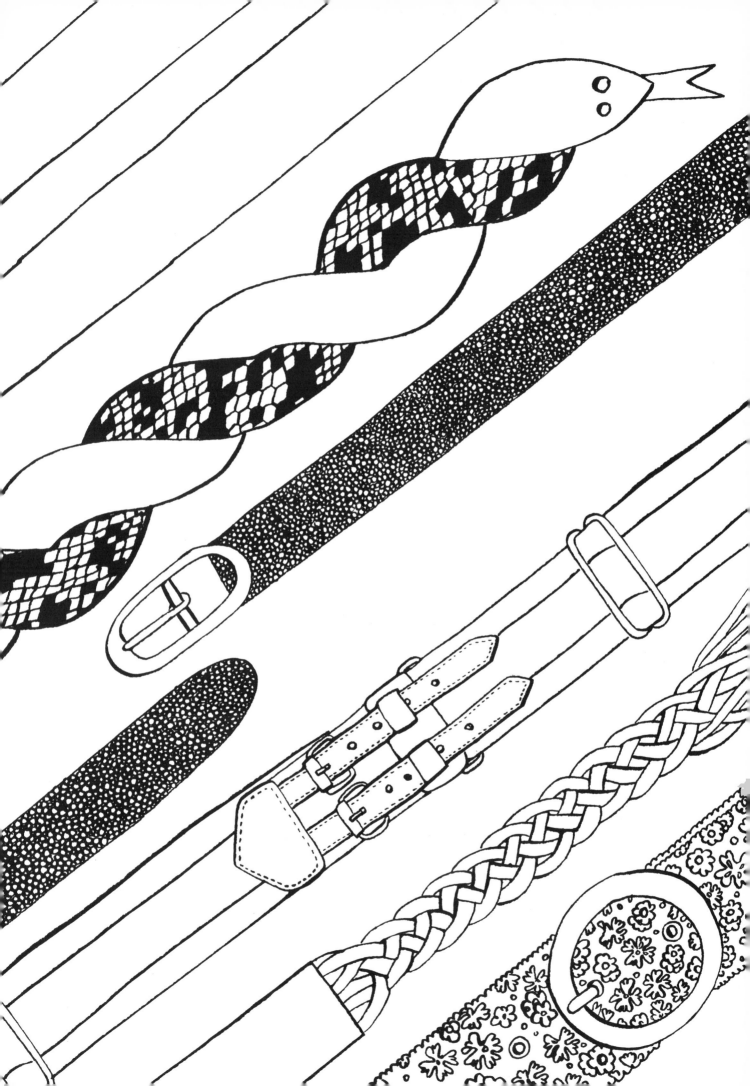

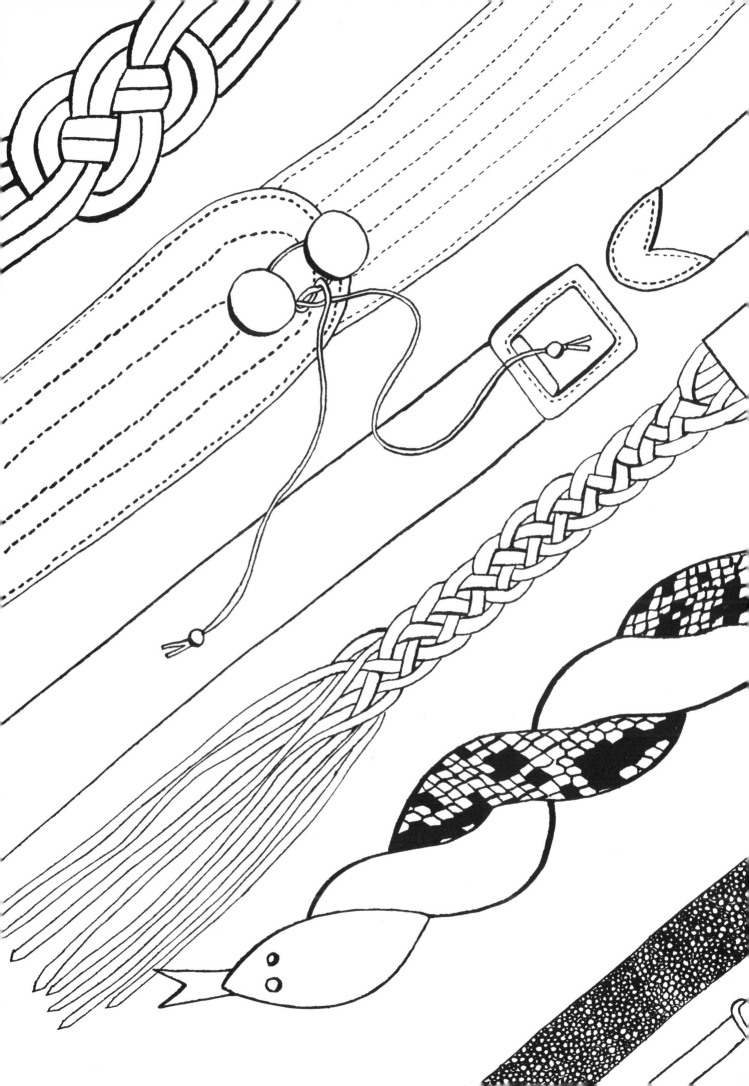

INUIT FASHION

IT'S COLD OUT THERE,
BUT WARM as TOAST IN HERE

HAIR HERO

MARSHA HUNT

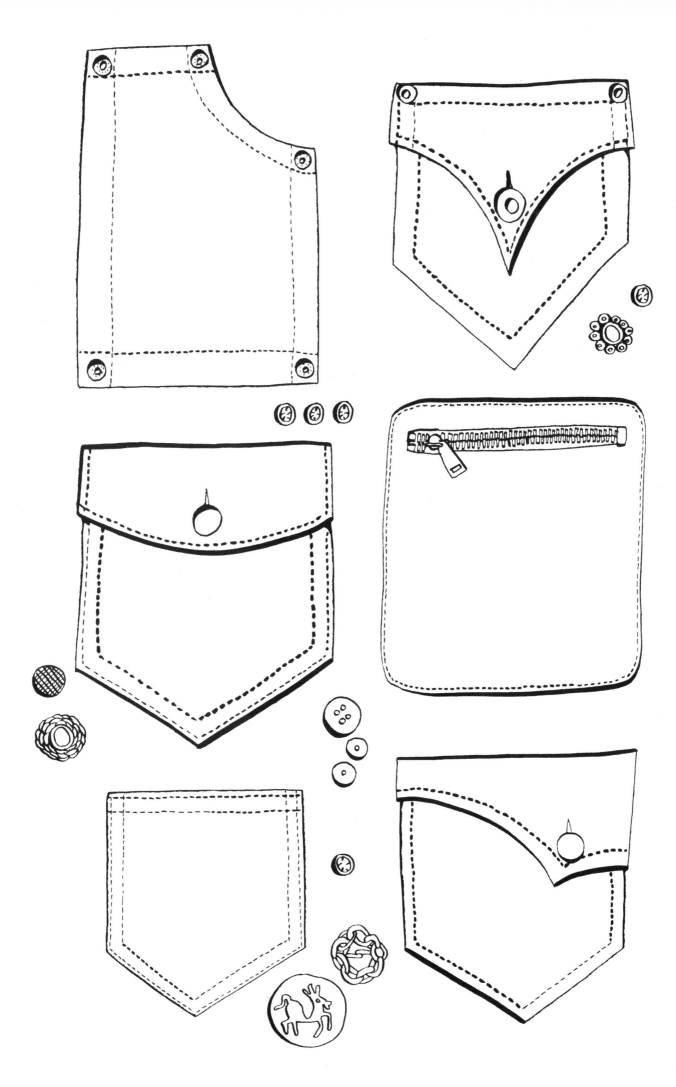

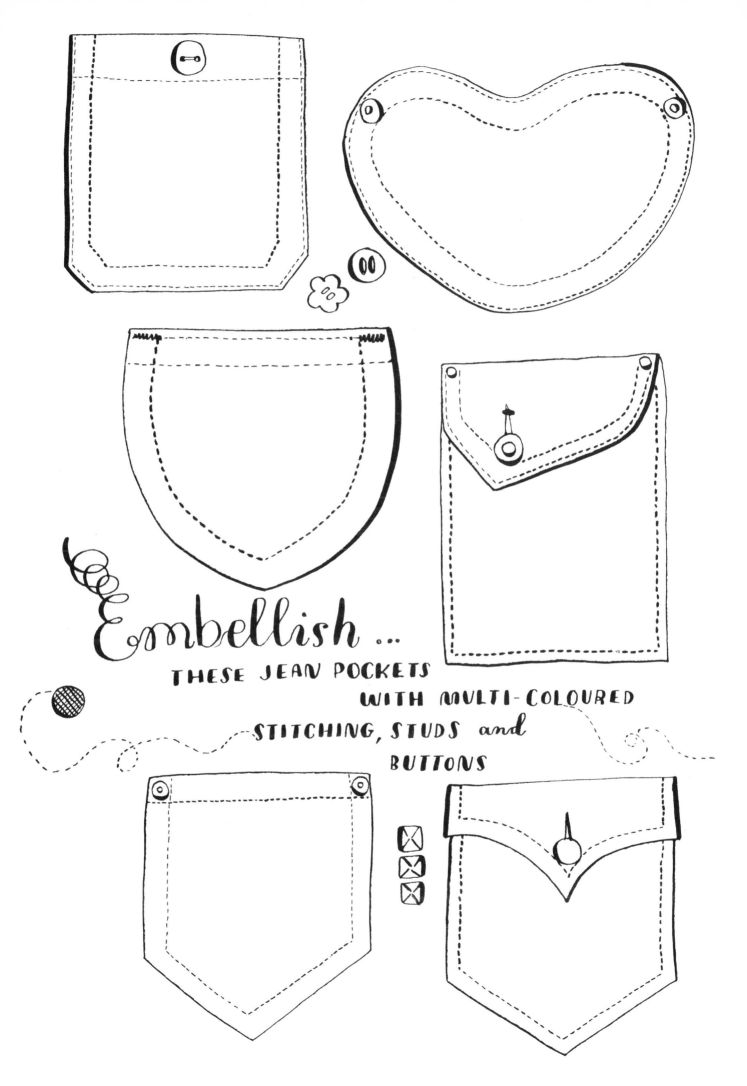

Embellish ...

THESE JEAN POCKETS
WITH MULTI-COLOURED
STITCHING, STUDS and
BUTTONS

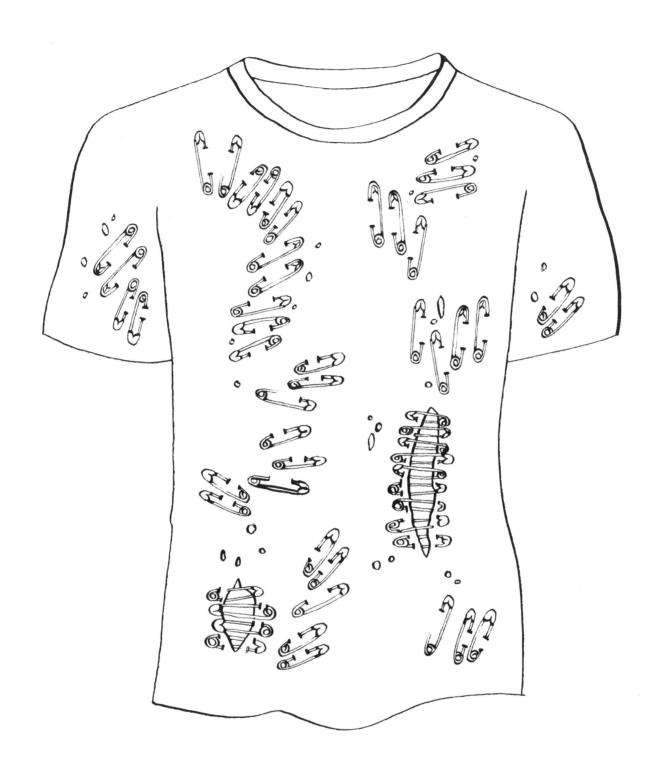

GIVE an OLD T-SHIRT
A NEW LIFE BY
COVERING IT WITH
SAFETY PINS

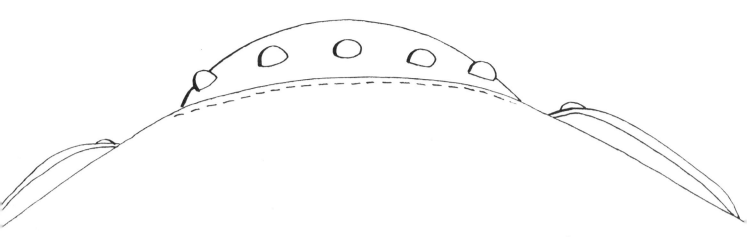

TRANSFORM THE BACK OF THIS JACKET
WITH STUDS and SEQUINS

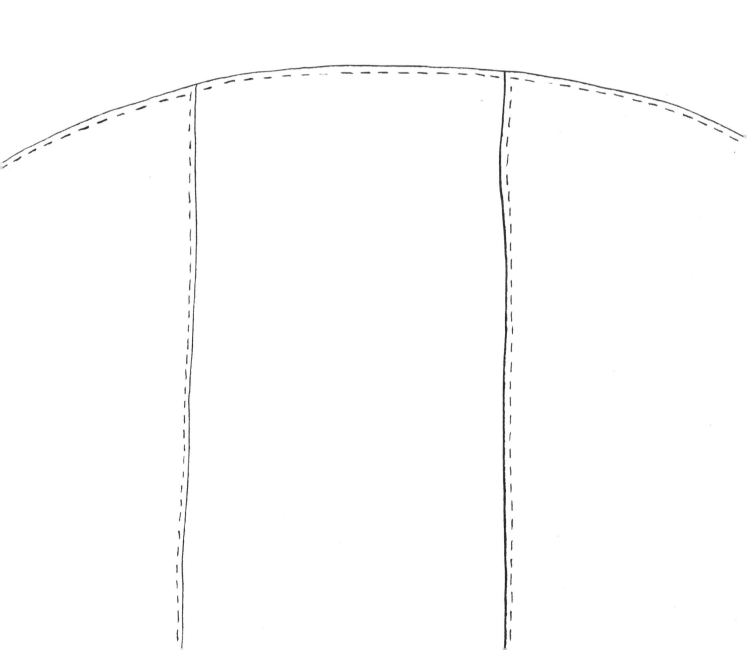

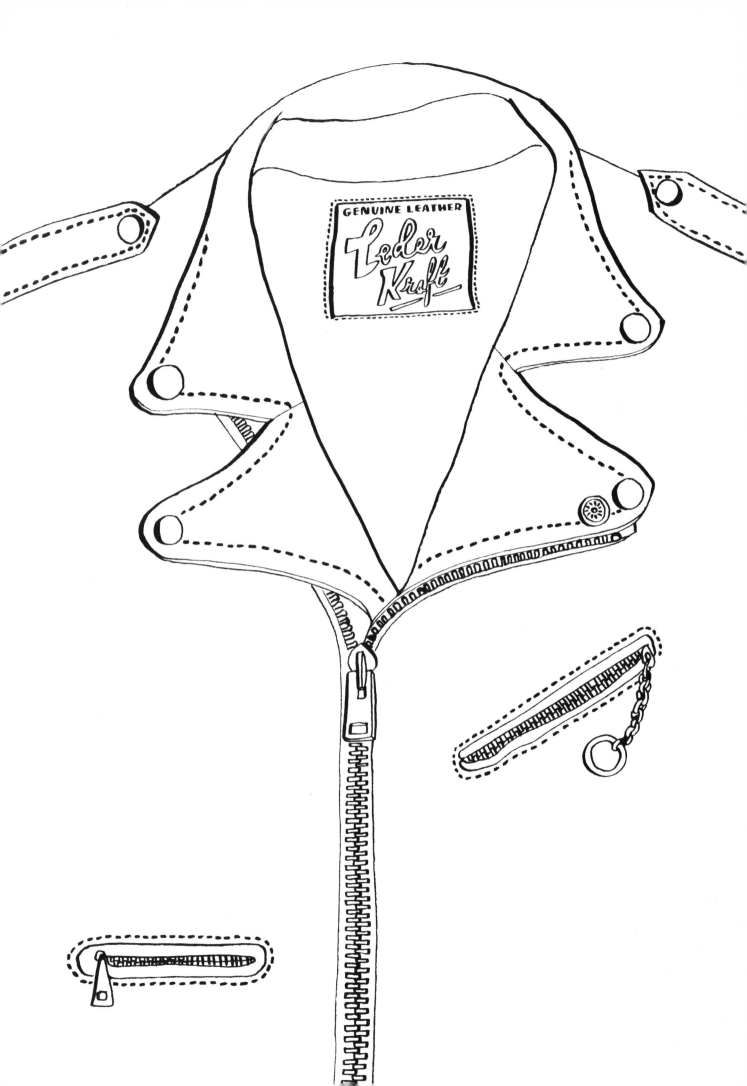

USE THESE STUDS, PATCHES and BADGES TO CUSTOMIZE THE JACKET OPPOSITE

USE A FAVOURITE
ANIMAL OR BIRD AS
INSPIRATION
TO DESIGN YOUR
OWN HANDBAG

FASHION ARCHIVE

JUDITH LEIBER

OFTEN USES
ANIMALS AND BIRDS
AS INSPIRATION FOR
MAKING INCREDIBLE
HANDBAGS

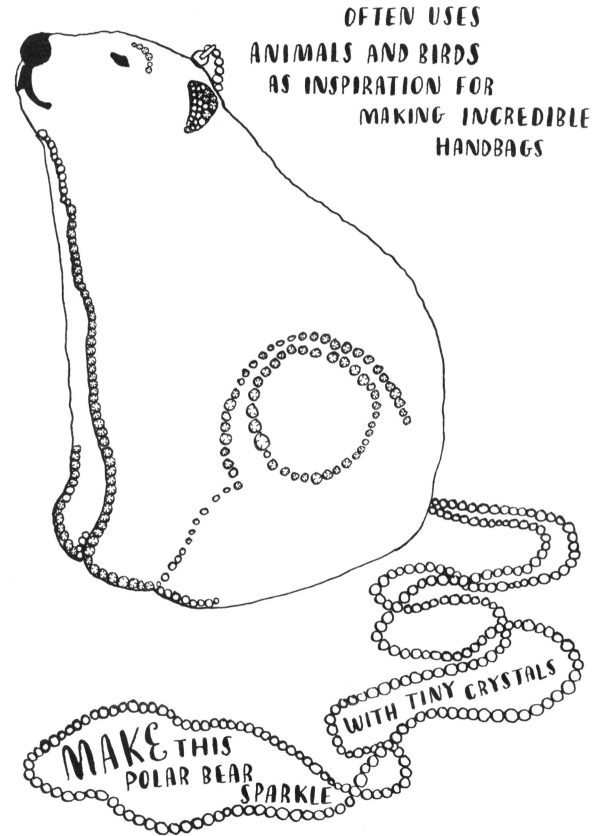

MAKE THIS POLAR BEAR SPARKLE WITH TINY CRYSTALS

INVENT YOUR OWN PATTERN
FOR THIS CHULLO HAT

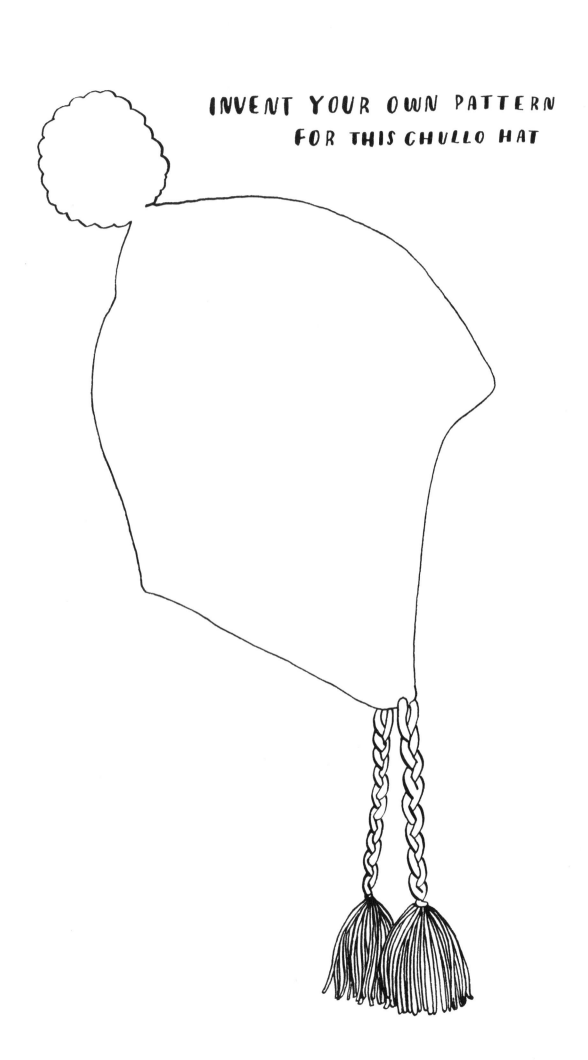

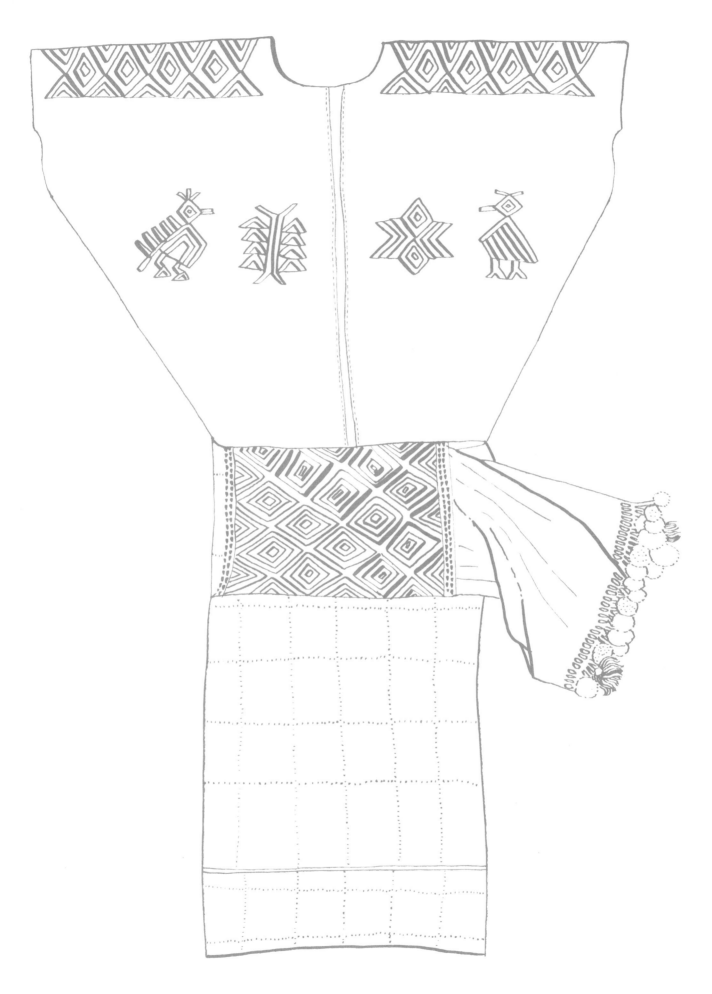

A DRESS FROM GUATEMALA

draw A FACE TO FIT THE BOB

DRAW CLEOPATRA A HEADDRESS
FIT FOR A QUEEN

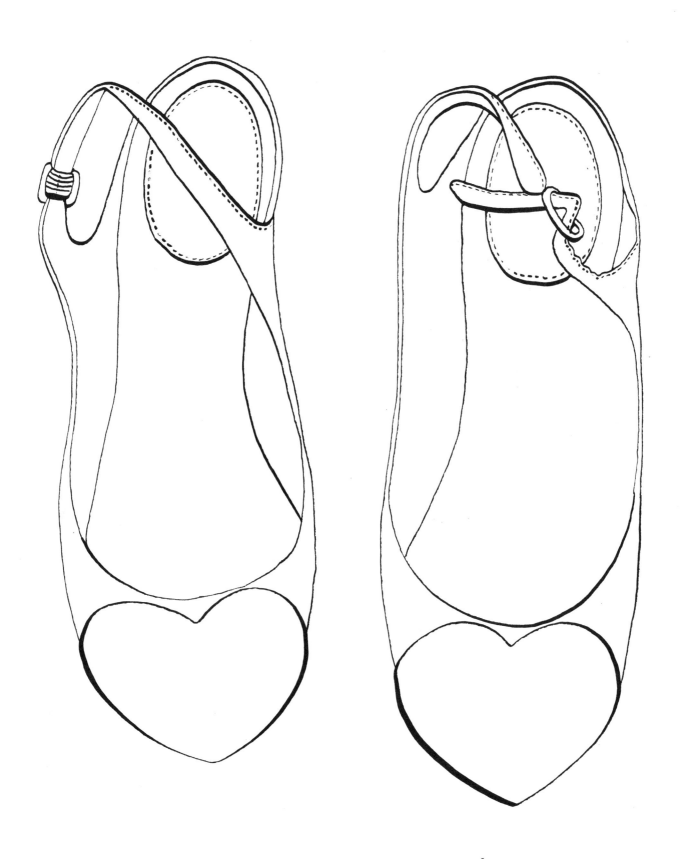

I HEART MY FRIEND IZZIE'S SHOES
COLOUR THEM PINK and RED

DRAW A HAIRBAND FOR THIS BOW

DRAW SHOES FOR THE BOWS

DRAW A PRETTY BOW ON EACH GLOVE

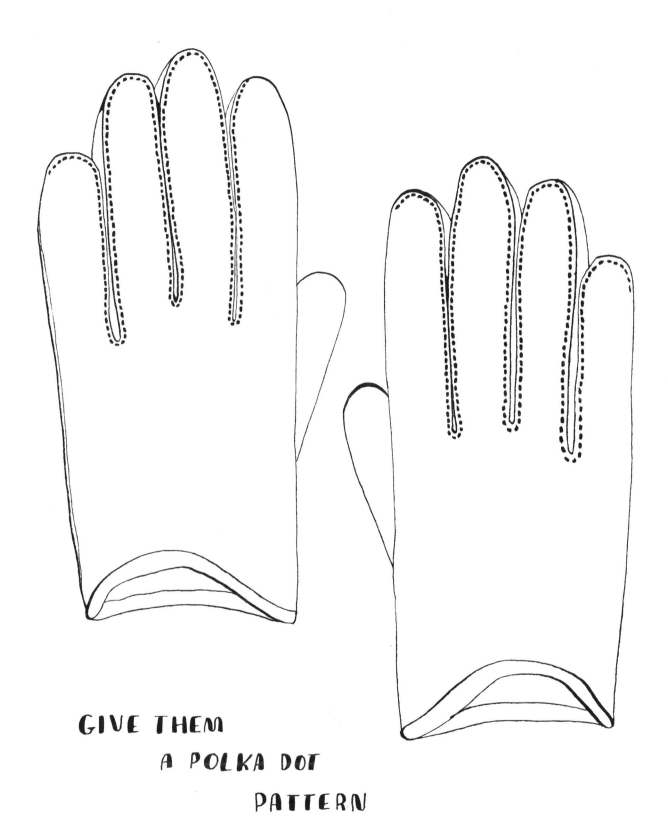

GIVE THEM
    A POLKA DOT
        PATTERN

JUST WHO IS WEARING THESE DARING SHADES?

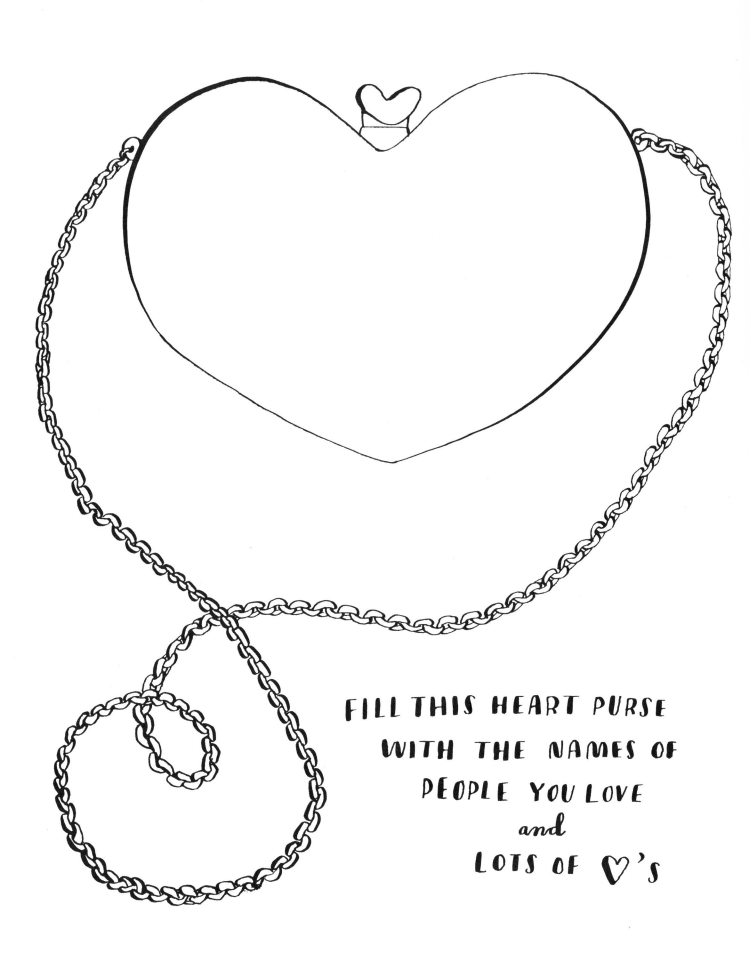

FILL THIS HEART PURSE
WITH THE NAMES OF
PEOPLE YOU LOVE
and
LOTS OF ♡'s

FASHION ARCHIVE

JEAN DESSÈS

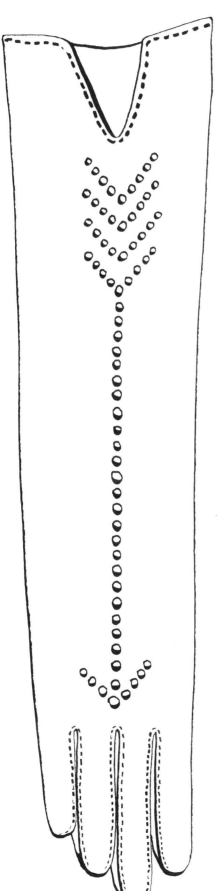

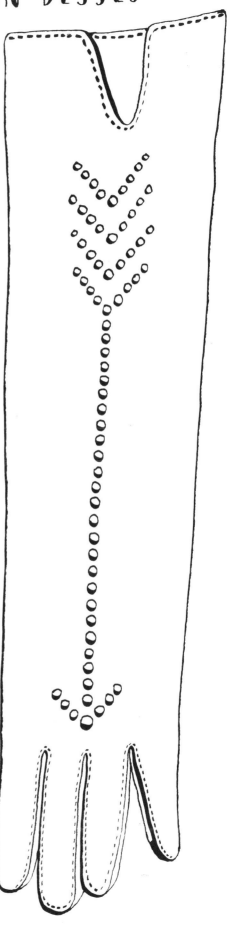

RHINESTONE STUDDED
EVENING GLOVES, 1950's

DRAW A DOTTY PAIR OF SHOES

ADD SOME MORE SEQUINS TO THIS DRESS

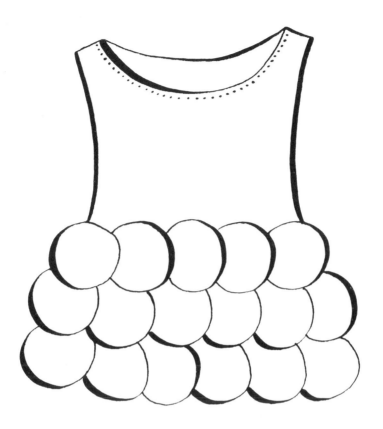

PAINT EACH SEQUIN A
DIFFERENT COLOUR FOR a
STUNNING CREATION

DRAW YOURSELF ON THIS PAGE
AND DRESS UP USING ANY OF THE
ITEMS ON THE PAGE OPPOSITE

I WOULD NEVER BE SEEN IN............-

DRAW THE BAG
ATTACHED TO THE CHAIN

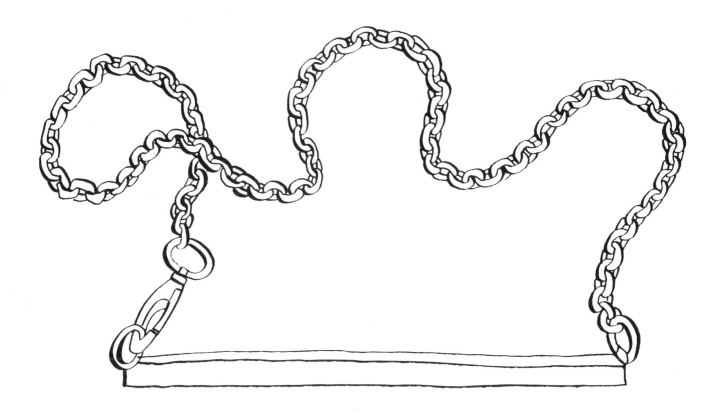

JUDY BLAME USES BUTTONS, SAFETY PINS and TRINKETS TO CREATE SOMETHING ENTIRELY UNIQUE

" I CAN MAKE SOMETHING FROM ANYTHING AND I SEE BEAUTY IN EVERYTHING "

TAKE ONE PLAIN COIN PURSE...

... AND TURN IT INTO
SOMETHING EXTRAORDINARY

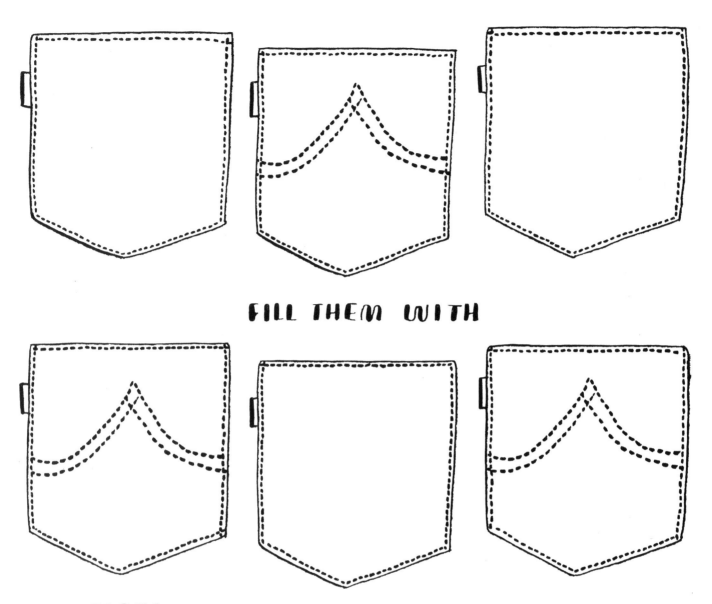

FILL THEM WITH

FACES, DOODLES and WHATEVER YOU LIKE

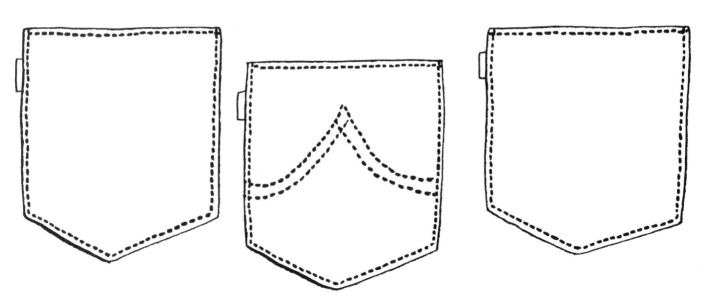

MAKE each OF THESE POCKETS

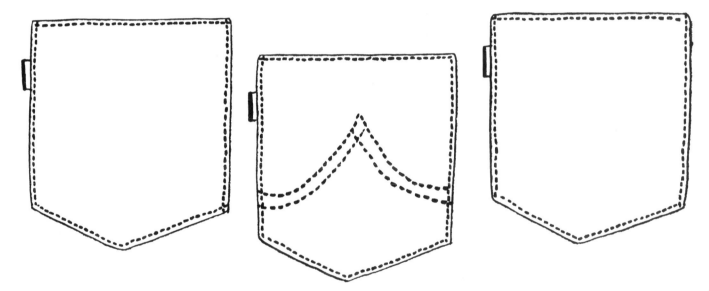

A MINI MASTERPIECE

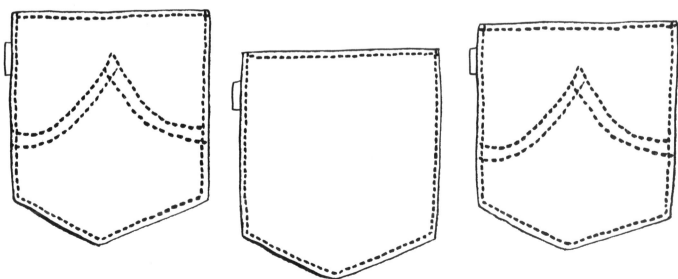

YOUR TURN !

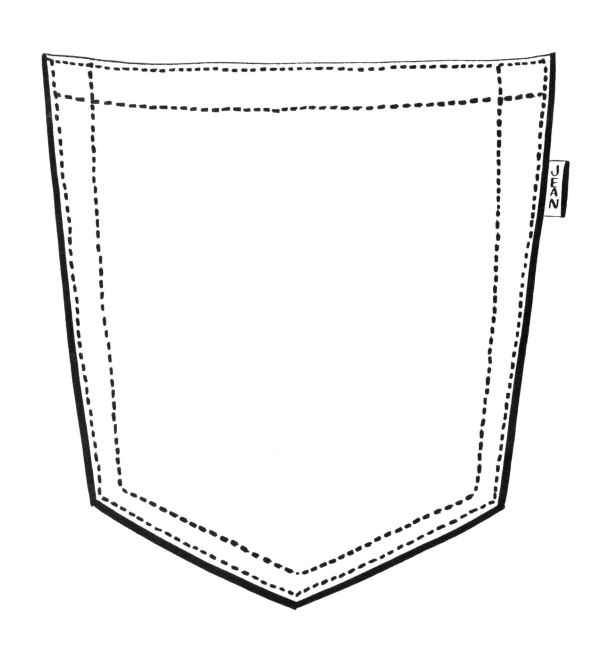

I PAINTED A FACE ONTO

MY JEAN POCKET

DRAW

SOMETHING MARVELLOUS

ONTO THIS JEAN POCKET

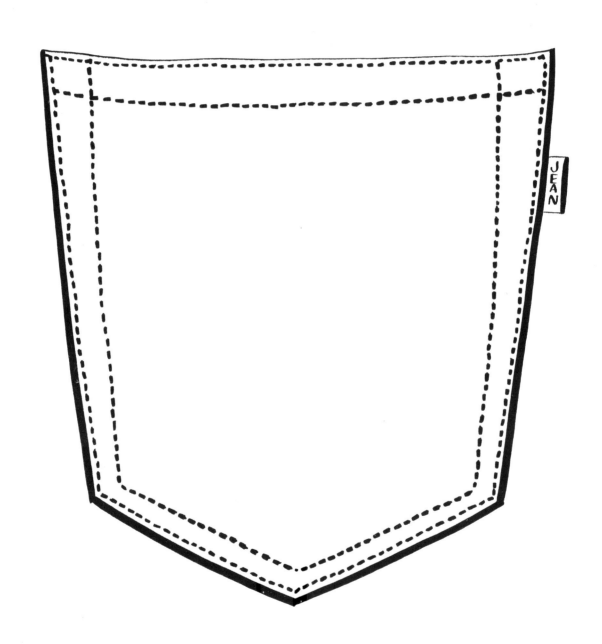

JEAN

DRAW

A LANDSCAPE

ONTO THIS JEAN POCKET

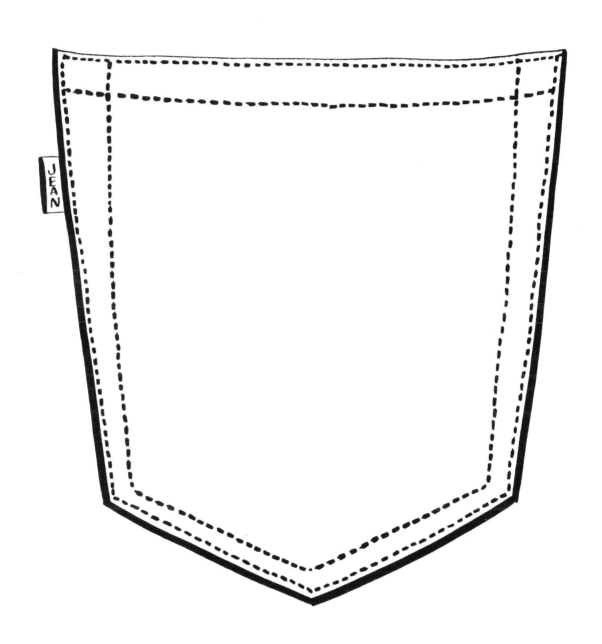

JEEPERS CREEPERS,

USE THESE

TO HIDE YOUR PEEPERS

QUEEN CLEOPATRA

LET YOUR IMAGINATION RUN WILD!

INSPIRED BY THEA'S SHOES
DESIGN SOME FANTASTICAL
SHOES OF YOUR OWN

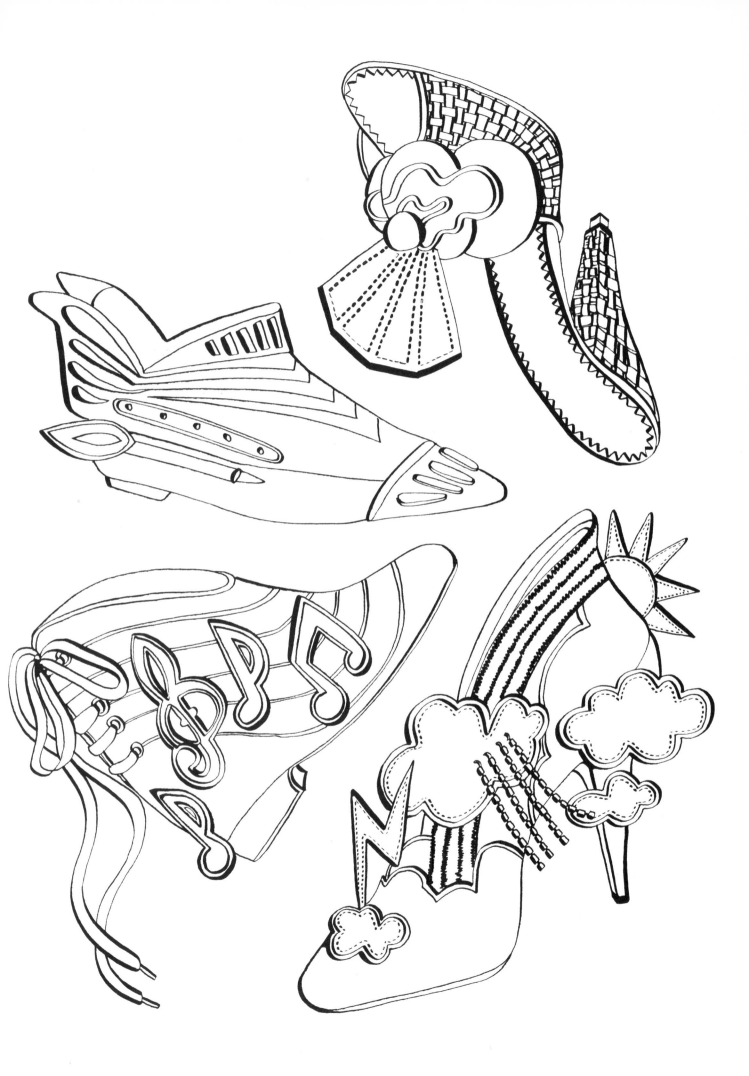

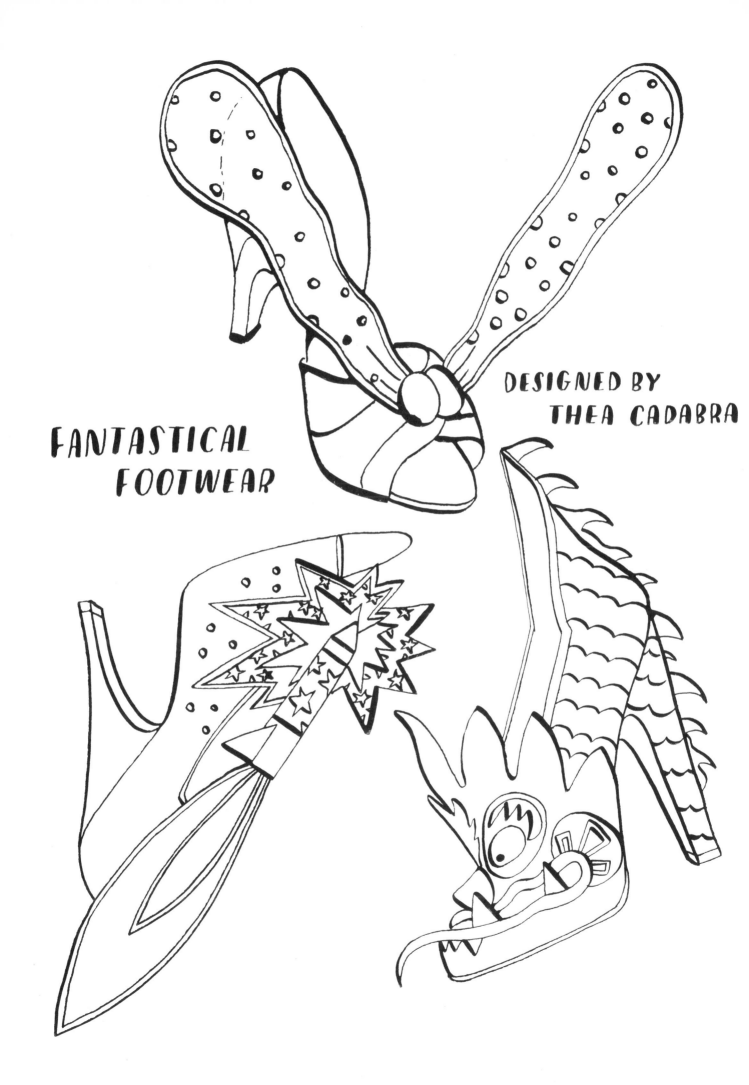

FANTASTICAL
FOOTWEAR

DESIGNED BY
THEA CADABRA

I WOULD NEVER WEAR ....

FASHION ARCHIVE

THE HERMÈS KELLY BAG

NAMED AFTER

THE ACTRESS

GRACE KELLY

COVER THIS ONE WITH GRAFFITI

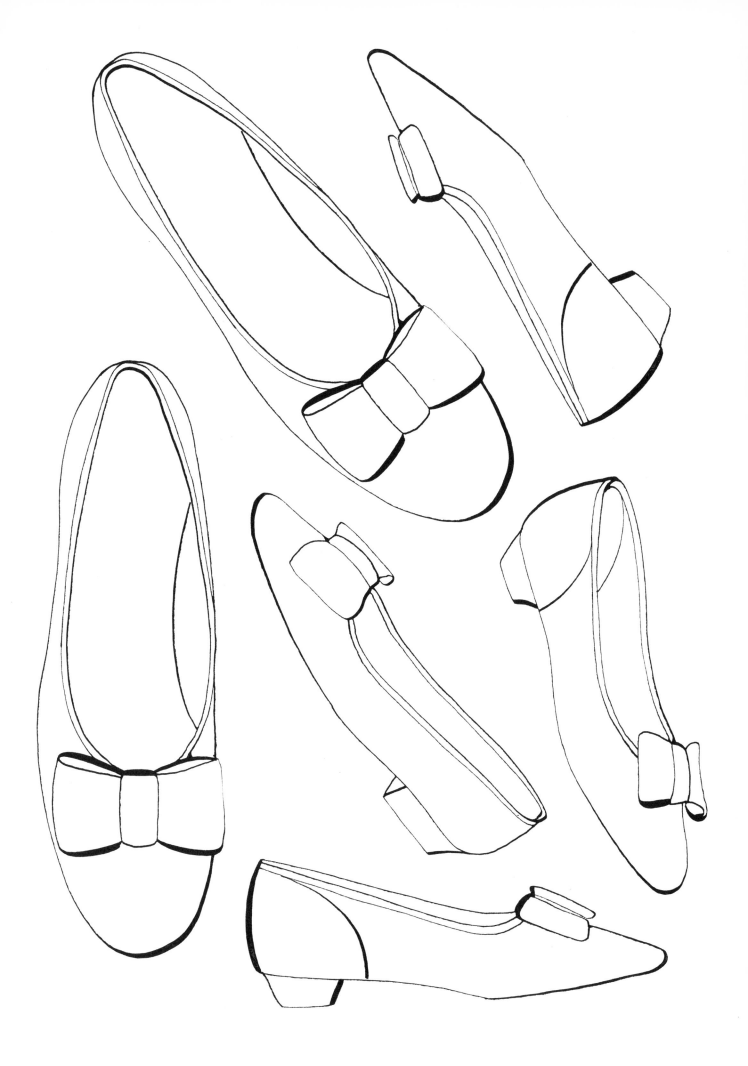

fill EACH SHOE
WITH A BEAUTIFUL
PATTERN

DRAW A FACE ON THIS PAGE
and ACCESSORIZE WITH
ANY OF THE ITEMS OPPOSITE

CLIP-ON EARRINGS

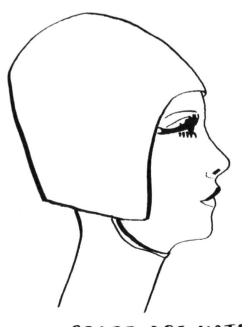

JACKIE "O" SUNGLASSES

BRIGITTE BARDOT EYES

TRIM
FITS
Tights

DARK 1

RUN RESIST

PANTYHOSE OR TIGHTS

SPACE-AGE HATS

FASHION FLASHBACK

THE 1960's

WHITE LIPSTICK

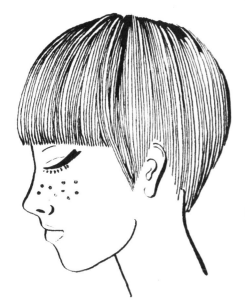

THE FIVE POINT BOB

PEACE PENDANT

GO-GO BOOTS

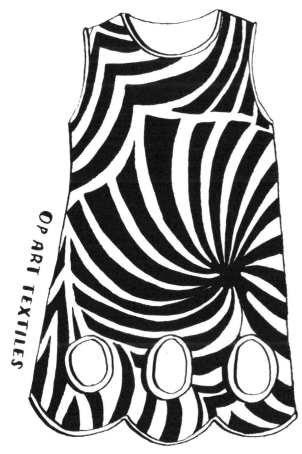

OP ART TEXTILES

PRINTED PAPER DRESSES

WHAT HAT WOULD YOU WEAR TO THE MOON?

Z Z Z Z Z

DRAW IT FOR ME PLEASE!

COVER THESE BOOTS
with
SHINY SEQUINS

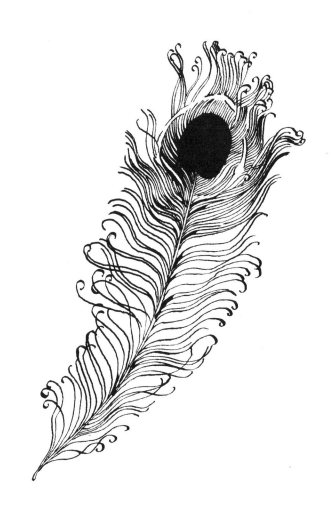

DRAW A BEAUTIFUL HAT
   FOR THE BEAUTIFUL FEATHER

FASHION ARCHIVE

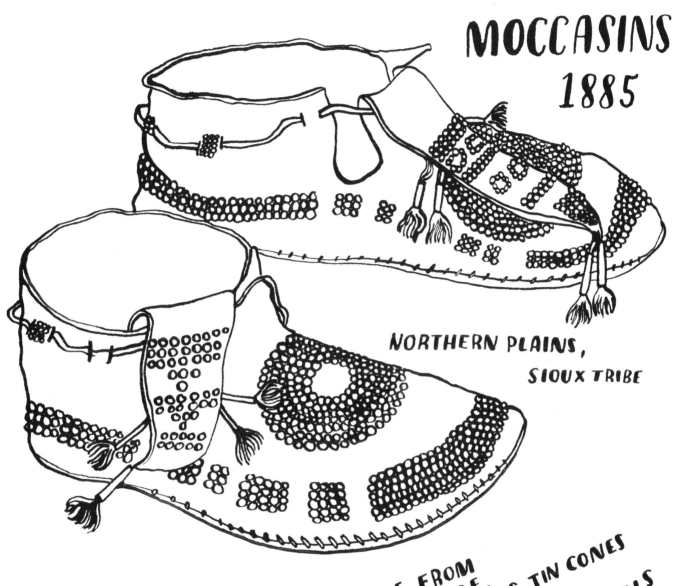

MOCCASINS
1885

NORTHERN PLAINS,
SIOUX TRIBE

MADE FROM
DEER HIDE,
GLASS BEADS, TIN CONES
RAWHIDE
and
PORCUPINE QUILLS

COLOUR IN THE BEADS

What
colours
will you
choose?

DESIGN YOUR OWN EARMUFFS

INVENT A PATTERN
FOR THE HEADBAND

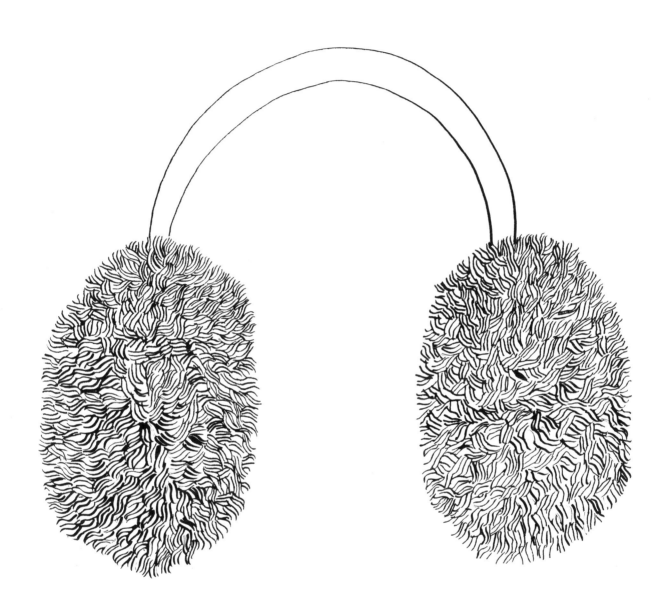

DRAW A FACE FOR
THESE FURRY EARMUFFS

FOLDING FANS OF SILK
WERE POPULAR IN THE 18th CENTURY

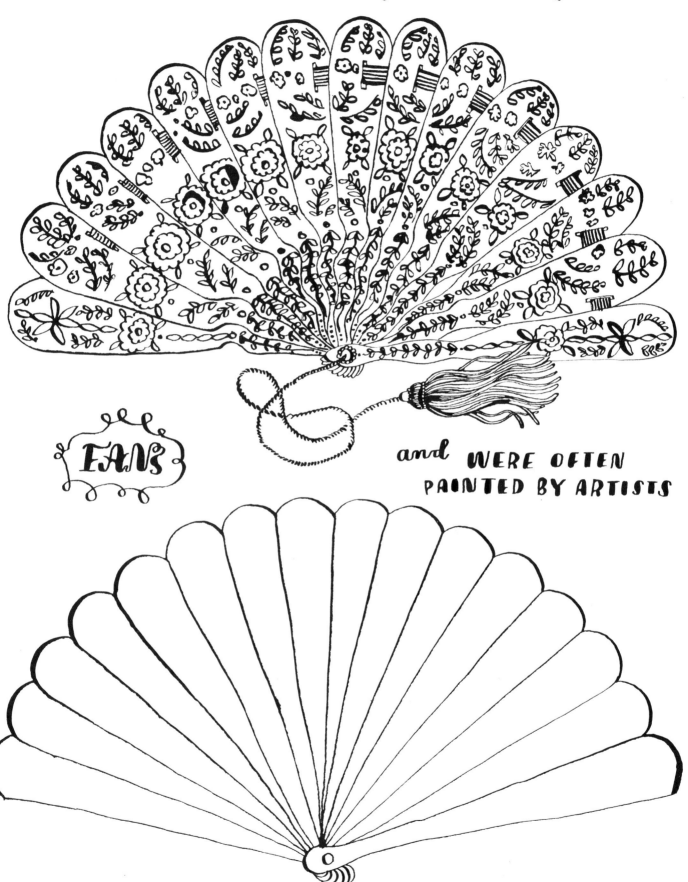

FANS

and WERE OFTEN PAINTED BY ARTISTS

HAVE FUN DECORATING THIS ONE YOURSELF

HAIR
HERO

Marie
Antoinette

HAVE FUN DRAWING HAIRSTYLES FOR THE LADIES

DRAW YOUR FANTASY HAIRSTYLE

DESIGN a
SPECTACULAR
PATTERN
FOR THESE
SOCKS

SOCK IT
TO ME !

DRAW BOWS ALL ALONG
THE SEAMS OF THESE STOCKINGS

DRAW YOURSELF ON THIS PAGE
AND DRESS UP USING ANY OF THE
ITEMS ON THE PAGE OPPOSITE

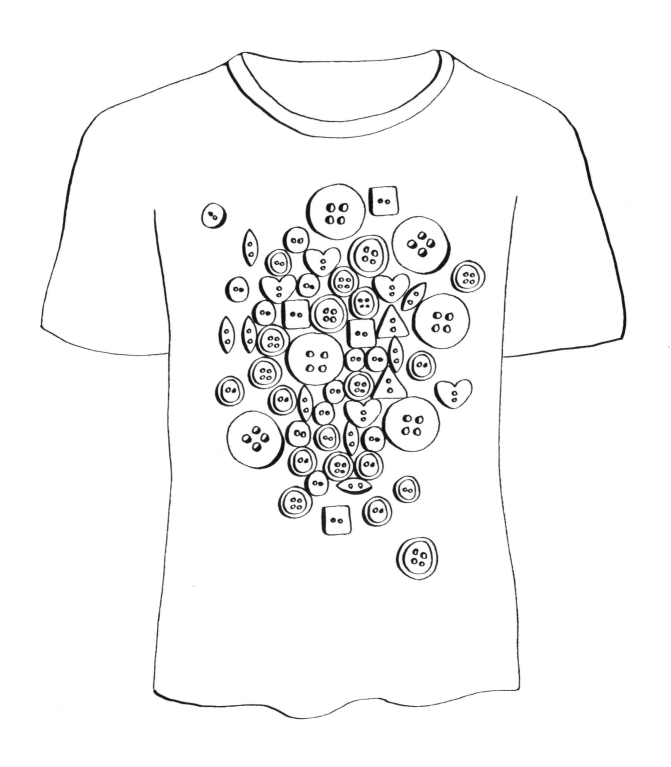

SEW BUTTONS

OF ALL SIZES and COLOURS

ONTO A T-SHIRT

TO CREATE A UNIQUE PIECE

GIVE THIS AMULET
an EXTRA-SPECIAL DESIGN

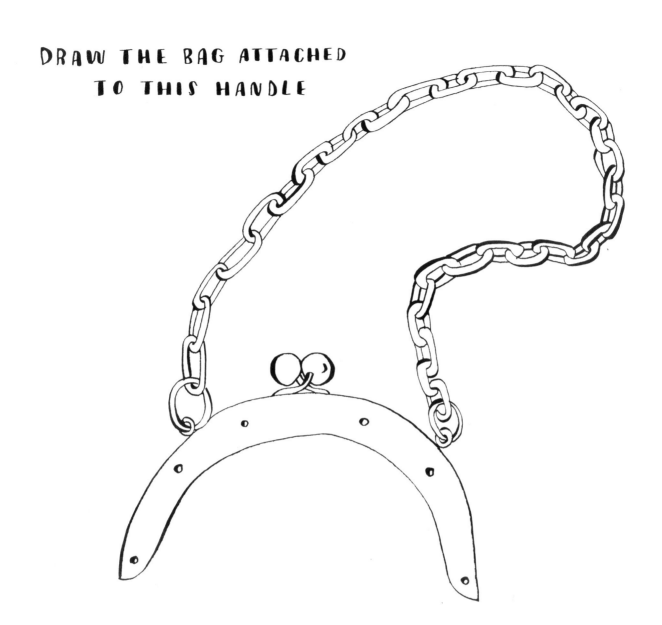

DRAW THE BAG ATTACHED
TO THIS HANDLE

DRAW A FANTASTIC COAT
FOR THIS SOPHISTICATED LADY

THE FRIENDSHIP BRACELET HAS ITS ORIGINS IN NATIVE AMERICAN TRADITIONS

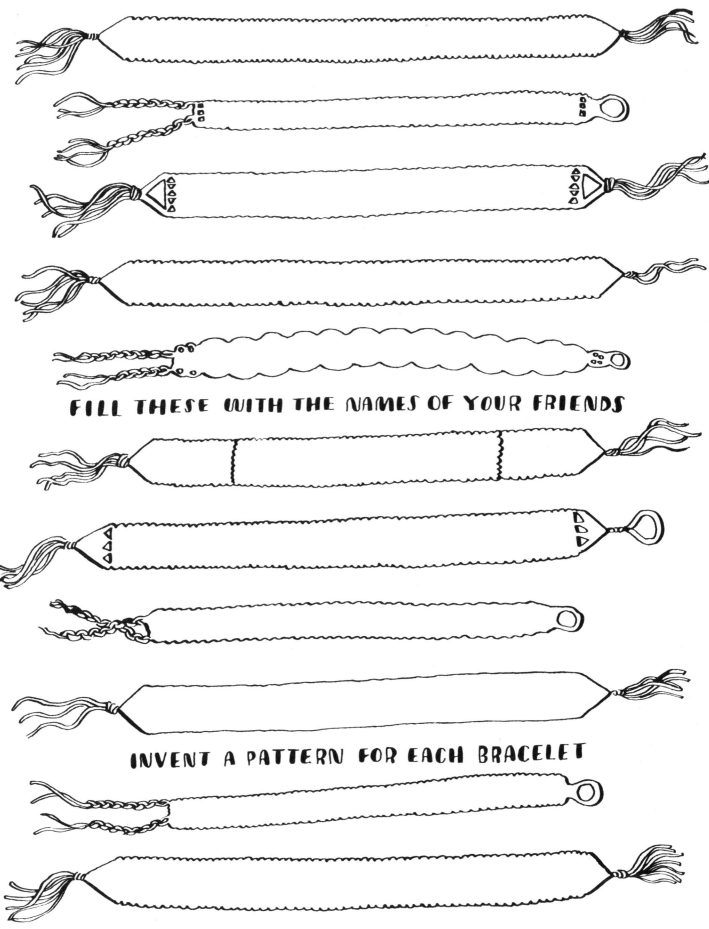

FILL THESE WITH THE NAMES OF YOUR FRIENDS

INVENT A PATTERN FOR EACH BRACELET

TASSELLED BELT
FROM
SACATEPÉQUEZ, GUATEMALA

DESIGN A BELT
THAT WOULD LOOK GOOD
WITH THESE SHOES

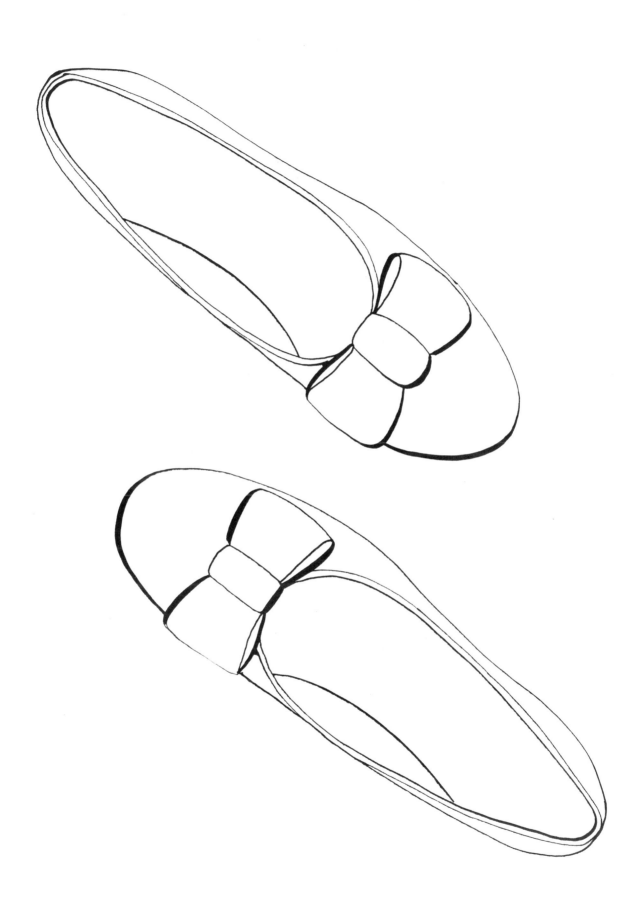

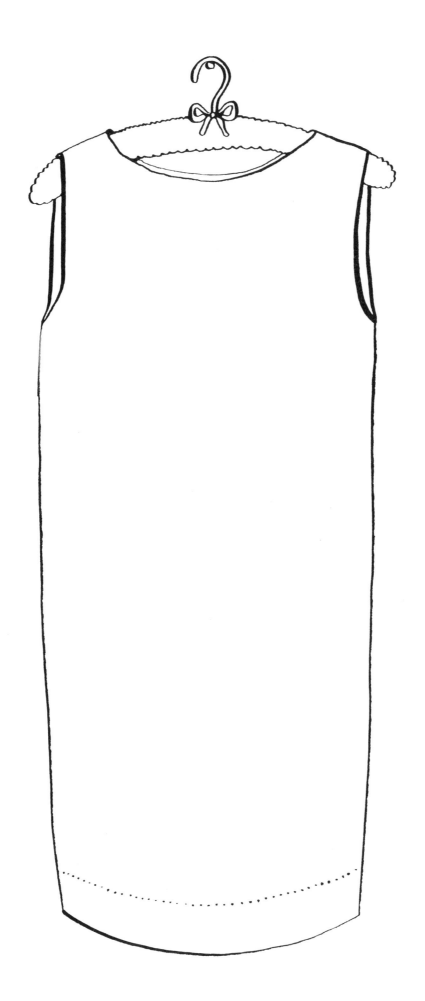

PRACTISE ON THESE ONES FIRST

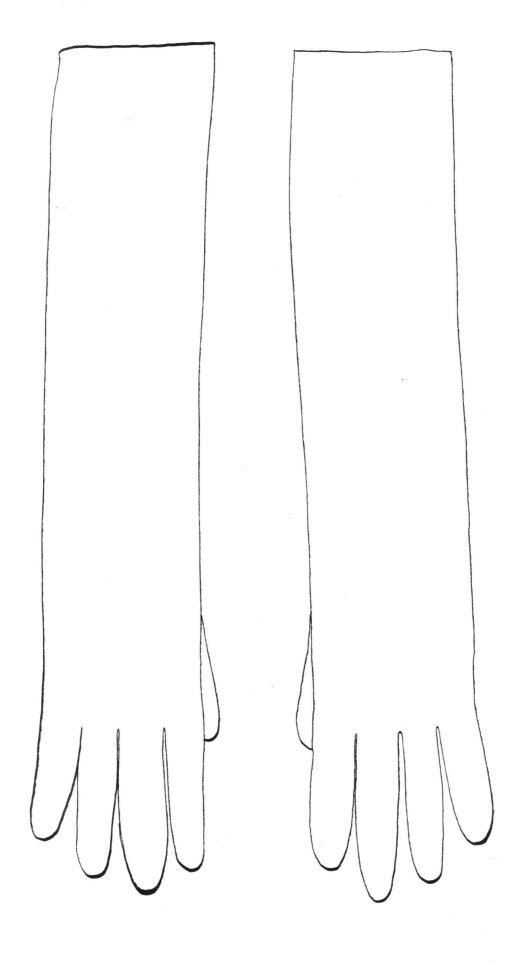

TOO YOUNG FOR A TATTOO ?

FIND SOME WHITE GLOVES AND GET CREATIVE WITH an INK PEN

DRAW YOURSELF ON THIS PAGE
AND DRESS UP USING ANY OF THE
ITEMS ON THE PAGE OPPOSITE

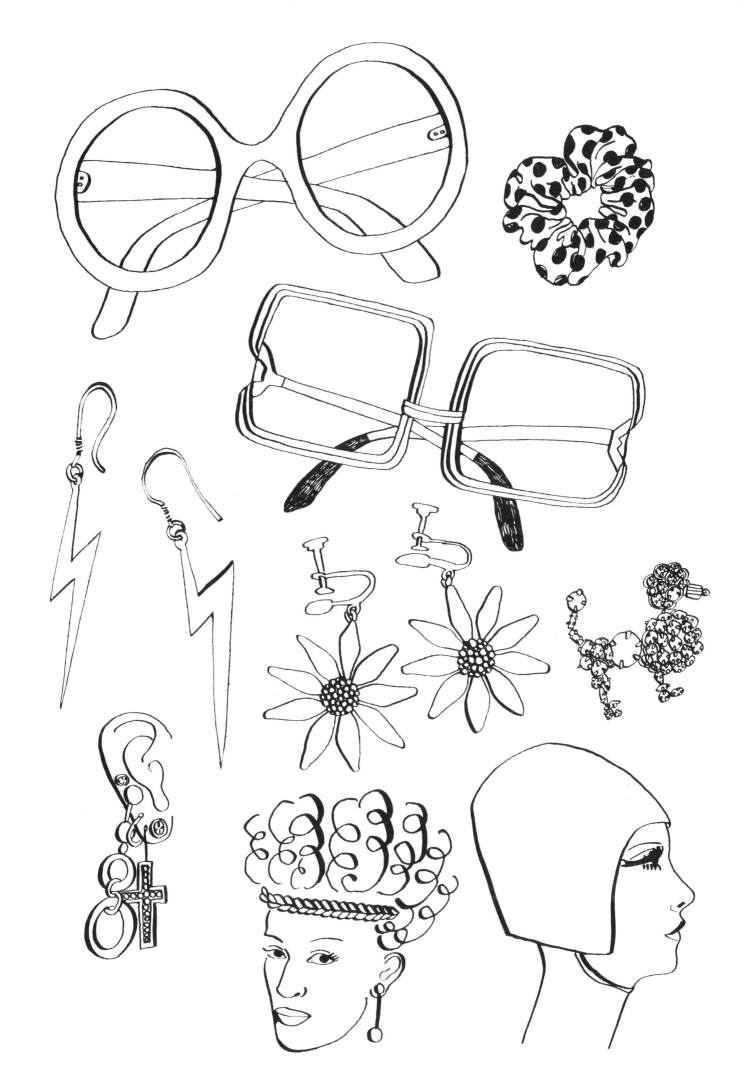

WHO IS WEARING
THESE EARRINGS ?

HOW ABOUT DRAWING
A NECKLACE TO MATCH ...

PARIS, MILAN, MOZAMBIQUE...

THE WORLD IS YOUR OYSTER !

MAKE A LABEL FOR
EACH ONE
OF YOUR BOUTIQUES

MAKE EACH ONE

ORIGINAL and BEAUTIFUL

OSSIE CLARK PARIS

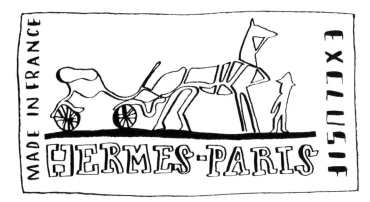

MADE IN FRANCE

HERMES-PARIS

EXCLUSIF

Anglo Fabrics
® Boucanta
100% WOOL

100%
PURE
CASHMERE

97/38

MADE IN
SCOTLAND

BRAEMAR

Carnegie
MODEL

"IT'S A SYMPHONY"

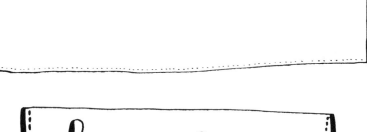

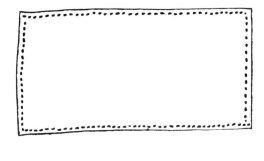

Adele Simpson

SOME MORE
LABELS FOR YOU
TO DESIGN

Schiaparelli

Paris

Levi Strauss
SPORTSWEAR
of California

HAND MADE IN AFGHANISTAN
EXCLUSIVELY FOR
HINDU KUSH
HAND WASH IN COOL WATER

MADE IN FRANCE SAINT LAURENT *rive gauche* PARIS

CHARLES JOURDAN
Paris

Harper's
WORCESTER

Classic
NOVVEAU BY
FIORUCCI

MADE IN
ITALY

MAKE EACH ONE
UNIQUE and SPECIAL

TED LAPIDUS
MADE IN ITALY

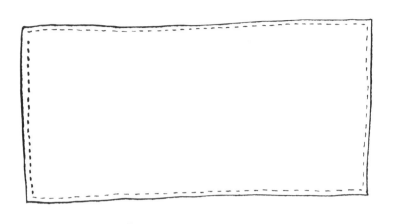

Salvatore Ferragamo
Firenze

St Michael
REGD
MADE IN GT. BRITAIN

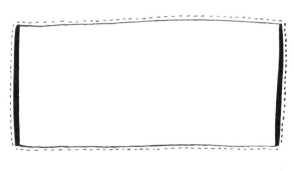

Tisse a Paris

POUR *Lilli Ann*
PARIS

INVENT YOUR OWN
FANTASTIC
FASHION LABELS

EMMANUELLE
KHANH PARIS

GEOFFREY BEENE

Made by
Shaheen's
of Ⓢ
HONOLULU

Marceline
MODEL
MADE AND DESIGNED IN DENMARK

JUTIK
MADE IN THAILAND, 100% COTTON
MACHINE WASH WARM, NO BLEACH

CREATE an INTERESTING CONTRAST

DRAW DOTS ONTO
THE SKIRT OF THIS
1950's COCKTAIL DRESS

COMPLETE the PATTERN ON THESE SUNGLASSES

STOCKINGS

NET PETTICOATS

FIGURATIVE JEWELLERY

PENCIL SKIRTS

BALLET FLATS

PEEP TOE SHOES

GIRDLE

COIFFURED HAIR

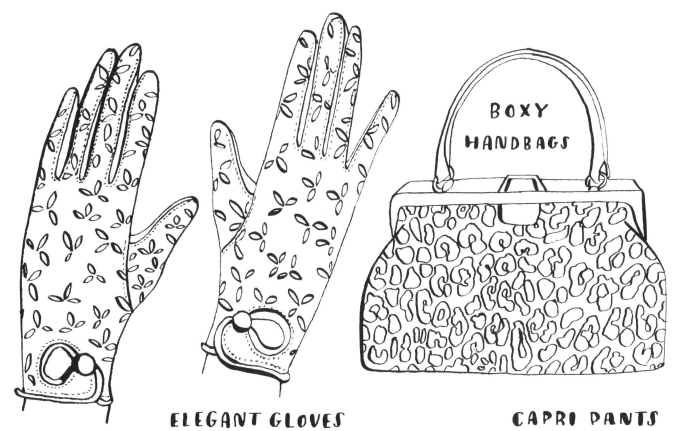

ELEGANT GLOVES

BOXY HANDBAGS

CAPRI PANTS

FASHION FLASHBACK

The 1950'S

WIDE BELTS

ESPADRILLES

CAT'S EYE SUNGLASSES

DRAW THE CENTREPIECE OF THIS TRIBAL NECKLACE

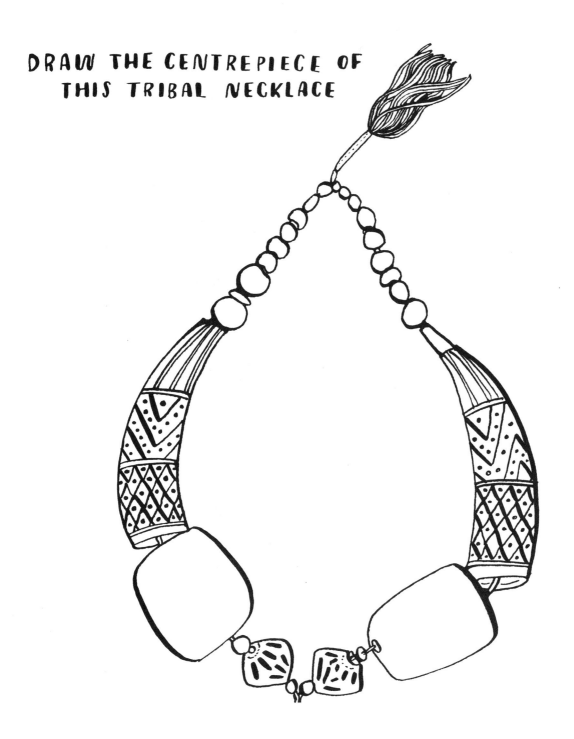

MAKE IT BOLD and BEAUTIFUL

BRIDAL
DRESS
IN DJIBOUTI,*
AFRICA

*IS IN BETWEEN
ERITREA,
ETHIOPIA
and
SOMALIA

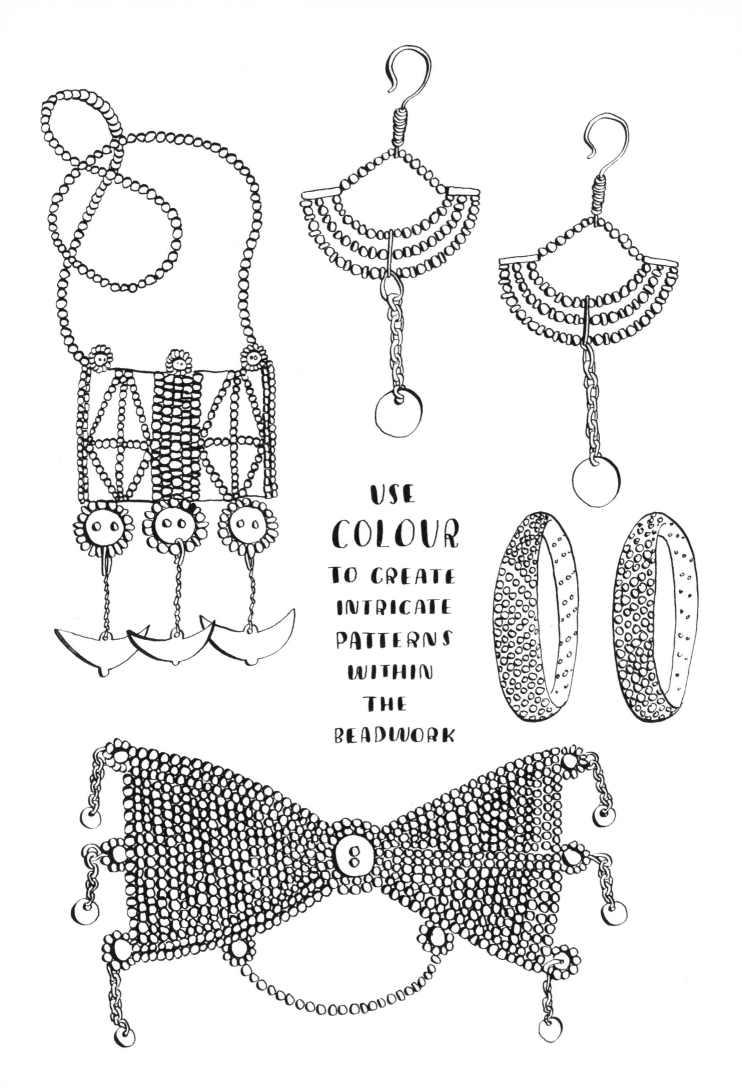

USE COLOUR TO CREATE INTRICATE PATTERNS WITHIN THE BEADWORK

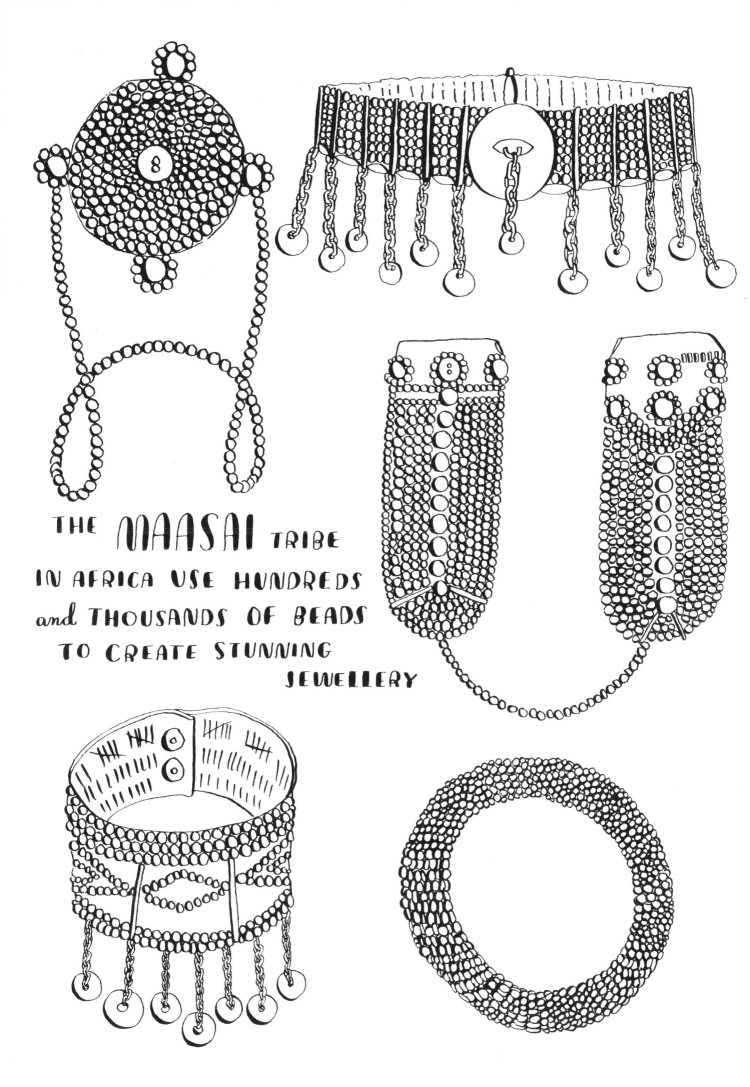

THE MAASAI TRIBE IN AFRICA USE HUNDREDS and THOUSANDS OF BEADS TO CREATE STUNNING JEWELLERY

DESIGN a BEAUTIFUL
PAIR OF SHOES
TO MATCH THE DRESS

FASHION ARCHIVE

THE *Cheongsam* WAS CREATED IN 1920's SHANGHAI

CREATE A DAZZLING PATTERN FOR THIS ELEGANT DRESS

FILL these PAGES
WITH YOUR DESIGNS
FOR BROOCHES

FANTASTIC
PLASTIC

Presenting...
THE INNOVATIVE JEWELLERY of
LEA STEIN

GIVE THIS ELEGANT MISS
A SWELLEGANT BEEHIVE DO

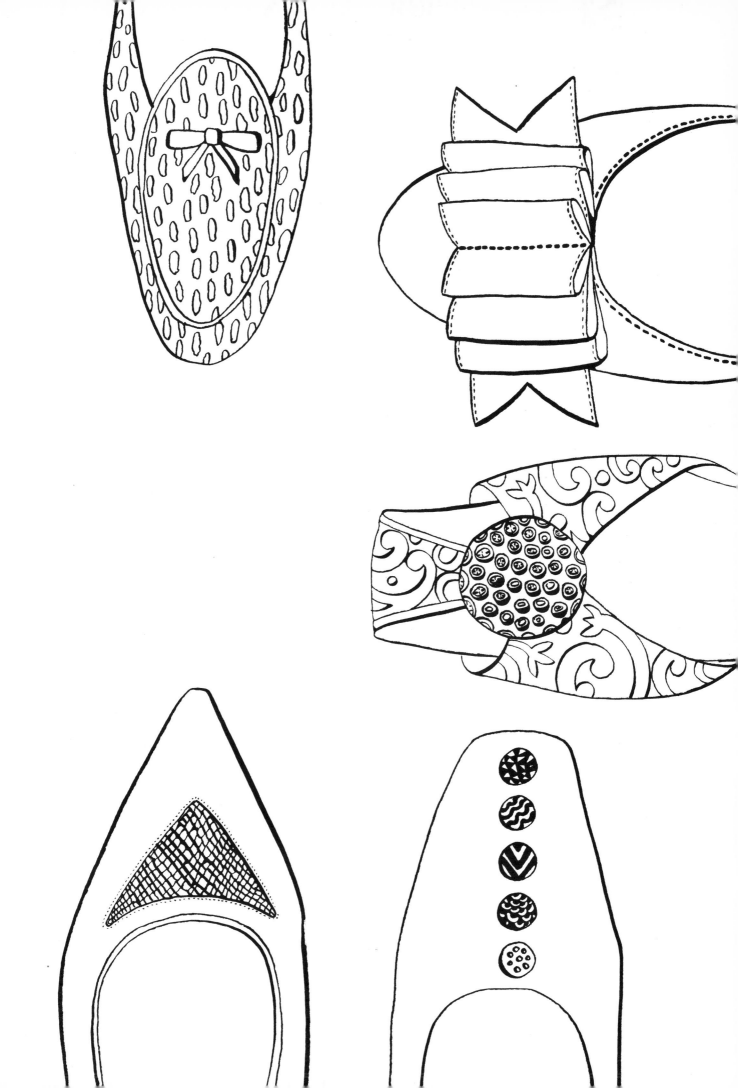

AN ORNATE MATADOR JACKET
CAN YOU COMPLETE the DESIGN ?

THE BOWLER HAT
CREATED IN BRITAIN IN THE 1880'S
FASHIONABLE AMONGST WOMEN IN BOLIVIA SINCE THE 1920'S

IT IS WORN PERCHED HIGH ON THE HEAD

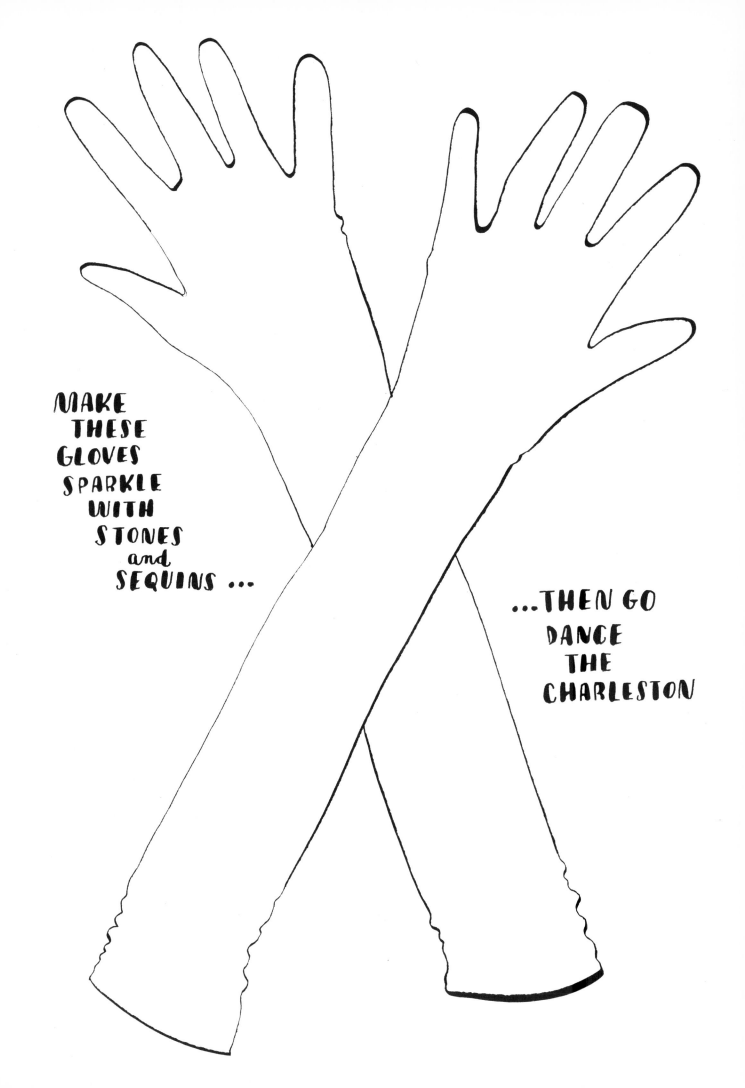

MAKE
THESE
GLOVES
SPARKLE
WITH
STONES
and
SEQUINS ...

...THEN GO
DANCE
THE
CHARLESTON

FILL these PAGES
WITH UNUSUAL, WITTY
and SCULPTURAL SHOES
OF YOUR OWN DESIGN

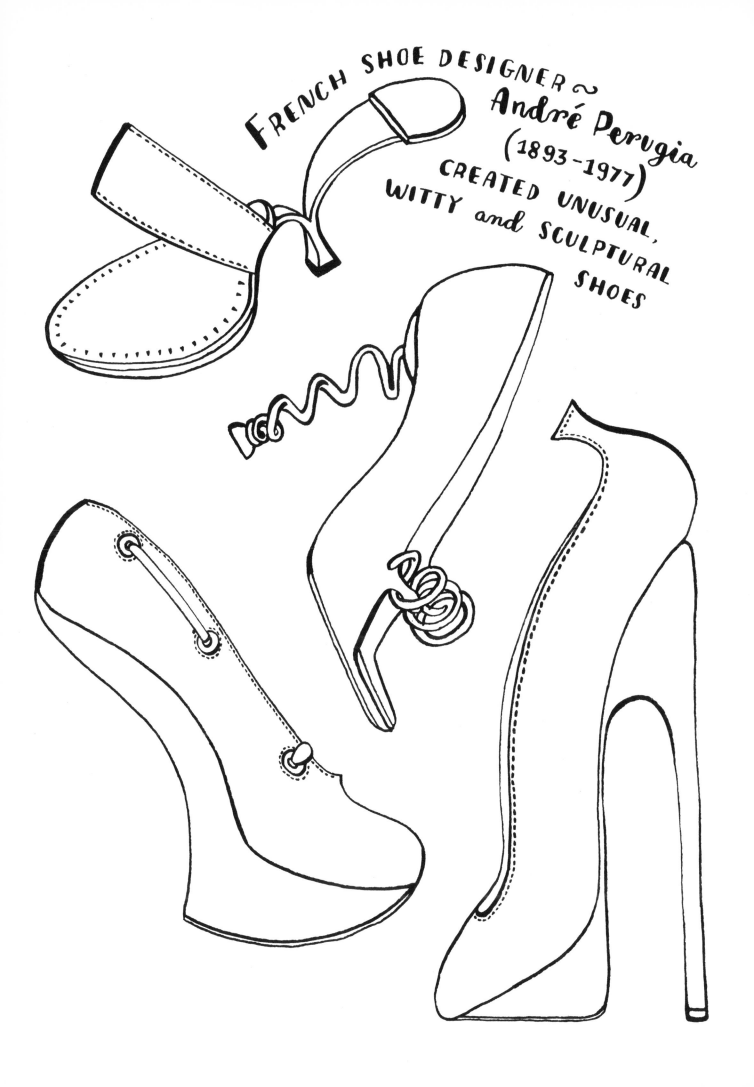

FRENCH SHOE DESIGNER ~ André Perugia (1893-1977) CREATED UNUSUAL, WITTY and SCULPTURAL SHOES

COMPLETE the PATTERN
ON THIS
HARLEQUIN MASK

DRAW THE FACE BEHIND THESE SHADES

*Your
imagination
is
your
reality*

DIANA VREELAND

MY EVEN MORE WONDERFUL WORLD OF FASHION

ANOTHER BOOK FOR DRAWING, CREATING and DREAMING

BY Nina CHAKRABARTI

LAURENCE KING PUBLISHING

LAURENCE KING

PUBLISHED IN 2011 BY
LAURENCE KING PUBLISHING LTD
361-373 CITY ROAD
LONDON EC1V 1LR
TEL + 4420 7841 6900
FAX + 4420 7841 6910
e-mail : enquiries@laurenceking.com
www.laurenceking.com

A CATALOGUE RECORD FOR THIS BOOK IS AVAILABLE
FROM THE BRITISH LIBRARY

ISBN-13: 978-1-85669-760-6

PRINTED IN CHINA

FOR
DIANE

MY
EVEN MORE
WONDERFUL
WORLD OF
FASHION

BELONGS TO :

SHOE SIZE:
